FROM
STUCK TO
SCALE

Overcome Obstacles to Achieve Breakthrough Business Growth

GRAMMAR

FROM STUCK TO SCALE

ANDREA KATES

Grammar Factory Publishing
MacMillan Company Limited
25 Telegram Mews, 39th Floor, Suite 3906
Toronto, Ontario, Canada
M5V 3Z1

www.grammarfactory.com

Kates, Andrea
From Stuck to Scale: Overcome Obstacles
to Achieve Breakthrough Business Growth /
Andrea Kates.

Paperback ISBN 978-1-998756-82-7

1. BUS063000 BUSINESS & ECONOMICS /
Strategic Planning. 2. BUS019000 BUSINESS
& ECONOMICS / Decision-Making &
Problem Solving. 3. BUS020000 BUSINESS
& ECONOMICS / Development / Business
Development.

Production Credits
Cover design by Designerbility
Interior layout design by Setareh
Ashrafologhalai
Book production and editorial services by
Grammar Factory Publishing

**Grammar Factory's Carbon Neutral
Publishing Commitment**
Grammar Factory Publishing is proud to
be neutralizing the carbon footprint of all
printed copies of its authors' books printed
by or ordered directly through Grammar
Factory or its affiliated companies through
the purchase of Gold Standard-Certified
International Offsets.

Disclaimer
The material in this publication is of the nature
of general comment only and does not represent professional advice. It is not intended
to provide specific guidance for particular
circumstances, and it should not be relied on
as the basis for any decision to take action or
not take action on any matter which it covers.
Readers should obtain professional advice
where appropriate, before making any such
decision. To the maximum extent permitted
by law, the author and publisher disclaim
all responsibility and liability to any person,
arising directly or indirectly from any person
taking or not taking action based on the information in this publication.

Praise for *From Stuck to Scale*

From Stuck to Scale sets the new gold standard for growth. Practical, original tools that address urgent challenges and equip corporate teams, entrepreneurs and ecosystem leaders to break through barriers and get unstuck. An inspiring industry leader, Andrea Kates applies decades of corporate insight to redefine how companies must innovate today. An eye-opening must-read and must-do.

JOHN METSELAAR, Leader Innovation & Transformation Institute, The Conference Board and Former CTO, P&G Brussels Innovation Center

Competitive advantage is a team sport in today's market, with innovation at its core. Andrea's *From Stuck to Scale* method gets leaders onto the same page about how to co-create bolder solutions to next-level challenges like circularity, infrastructure, and technology platforms, with a path for all types of talent to get on board.

FRANK BONAFILIA, Cofounder of the Edison Awards and the Lewis Latimer Fellowship

When it comes to growth in today's market, ecosystem activation is the critical ingredient. *From Stuck to Scale* provides a step-by-step guide to build a thriving ecosystem.

THOMAS KROGH JENSEN, CEO, Copenhagen Fintech

From Stuck to Scale saved our company, energized our team, and breathed a new sense of excitement into our investors, customers and suppliers.

NICOLAS CORTÁZAR, Director, Intergráficas

From Stuck to Scale brings a balance of Silicon Valley experience and global insight. What you get is a core set of tools that empower entrepreneurs in growth markets and equip leaders of global companies to build and sustain high-impact ecosystems.

DINA SHERIF, Executive Director, MIT Center for Development and Entrepreneurship

In *From Stuck to Scale,* Andrea Kates provides the operating system for organizational transformation: catalyzing the changemaker's mindset, developing the skill set for rapid scaling, and providing the flexible tool set to move from stasis to success.

GARY A. BOLLES, Global Fellow for Transformation, Singularity University

STEP 1 **ENVISION** 20

OVERCOMES "STUCK" AND BUILDS SKILLS IN THESE AREAS: Helps leaders become confident in imagining new possibilities, translating trends into value, and initiating change.

- **CASE IN POINT:** Nicolas Cortázar, Director, Intergráficas

- **TAKING STOCK:** Determine where your project, team, strategy and progress truly stand and what you'd like to tackle.

- **NOW/NEXT:** Create a snapshot of what the most powerful progress would look like.

- **SKETCH YOUR IDEA:** Build an expanded view of how your next steps could achieve broad impact.

- **FOUR QUADRANTS:** Engineer success in four dimensions: strong vision, engagement of talent, operations, and research/technology/data.

- **SPOTLIGHT STORY:** Shimizu

You can bring
ideas that matter
to millions of
people (but you
need new tools).

PROCESS

1 ENVISION	2 EXPAND	3 BUILD	4 ENGAGE	5 ACTIVATE
FOCUS: Clarify and express the essence of your next initiative	**FOCUS:** Apply fresh lenses: technology, cross-industry, business model, to go bolder	**FOCUS:** Make it real: learn, shift gears, modify and debug	**FOCUS:** Bring others into the fold. Internal, external, complementary, ecosystem	**FOCUS:** Enlist commitment. Operationalize the initiative. Build a thriving, evergreen system
>> Taking Stock >> Now/Next >> Sketch Your Idea >> Four Quadrants	>> 4-Beat Story >> Expanding the Story >> Innovation Enablers >> Opportunity Aperture >> Ideaboard	>> Ideaboard (Part 2) >> Experiment Tracker >> Untapped Opportunities >> Scale Optimizer >> Bias and Blind Spot Tracker	>> Commitment Narratives >> Impact Multiplier >> Ecosystem Mapper >> Transformative Leadership	>> 4-Beat Activation Story >> 4-Quadrant Activation Plan >> Activation Imperatives >> Culture of Activation >> Strategy Alignment

FOREWORD BY JOHN METSELAAR

Leader Innovation & Transformation Institute,
The Conference Board and Former CTO, P&G
Brussels Innovation Center

WHEN ANDREA TALKED to me and presented me with the honor of writing the foreword for her new book, it took me a while to strategize how to connect my experiences with her core message and the powerful underlying concepts. Eventually, it brought me back to my almost thirty years of leading innovation at Procter & Gamble, which ended ten years ago.

The interesting thing with a single-company career, I now know, is that you take certain things for granted as "universally accepted" or "the way" everywhere. For instance, "innovation is our lifeblood," "consumer is boss," or considering sustainability to be a three-legged stool, where 1) the financial leg, 2) the environmental leg, and 3) the social leg needed to be equal for the stool to be stable.

Another "given" was the statement we lived at P&G that "execution is the only strategy the consumer ever sees," which led to a focus and commitment—an obsession almost—that our ideas saw the light of the marketplace day, with excellence. And we were organized, motivated, and trained to achieve exactly that—underpinning, I believe, 187 years of business success.

Then, after I retired from the company, I found myself in the big wild world of innovation, leadership, strategy, and culture as a professor of management practice at the Solvay Brussels School (ULB) and as leader of The Conference Board's Global Innovation & Digital Institute. I then got to talk to thousands of business and innovation leaders across companies, industries, and regions of the world, and I now know that the real world is very different from my earlier, myopic perspective.

Maybe my biggest "aha!" has been how the business world is struggling with the notion of innovation, even starting from what innovation means, or is. Too many people associate it single-mindedly with creativity. Their obsession with brainstorming turned into hackathons, post-its, bean bags and table tennis outfits.

But, in reality, as one key statement in my Leading & Living Innovation university course goes: "Innovation is one percent inspiration, ninety-nine percent perspiration." The ideation work is the easy part; ninety-nine percent of sweat goes into turning the idea into successful market execution, and commercialization, at scale. This is a long, tedious, rocky, and uncertain path from ideation to in-market success—through conceptualization, exploration, qualification, production readiness, quality insurance, and commercial readiness. So, too many business leaders fall victim to what's being called "innovation theatre": showing stakeholders, boards, and investors pictures of the hackathons to suggest they're leading with innovation.

Let's step back to understand what innovation is, fundamentally. The definition I use in class, and which I love for its punch and completeness, is: "Innovation converts inspiration and knowledge into new value." The inspiration, indeed, is there and needs to be intersected with effective knowledge build and management, but it is that conversion element that is the bottleneck in the creation, and capture, of new value. The mindset may not be on growth, but more fixed on "let's not rock the boat, we've always been successful like this." The process may be suboptimal (or absent). The organization may not be in place to allow for the multifunctional teamwork that's required. The systems may hurt rather than help. The culture may be fearful of failure rather than open to curiosity, experimentation and learning (including failing). In reality, there are critical junctures where everyone gets stuck, and sadly, teams are left without a roadmap to move forward.

This is where I introduce Andrea Kates into the story. Andrea and I met a few years ago when we both spoke at an event. After we finished our presentations, we were each impressed and explored how our common ground of technology, strategy and practical application might combine to move companies forward. As our relationship developed, I invited Andrea to serve as Senior Fellow for The Conference Board, where she brings a rich combination of research savvy as well as practitioner insight.

Every time Andrea writes a research paper—like the ones she's co-authored on regional fintech and innovation ecosystems—she brings a brilliance in coming up with original models that translate thorny issues into how-tos. Every time Andrea is in front of an audience, whether it's a group of corporate leaders around a table or presenting a keynote, she impresses everyone with her no-nonsense, action-oriented, practical principles and tools to help generate new value at scale into the market. From artificial intelligence (AI) to strategic ecosystems to fintech to manufacturing to circular economy issues, Andrea cuts to the chase and helps leaders apply innovation in practical ways.

This new book, *From Stuck to Scale*, pulls Andrea's talents and original thinking into a treasure recipe to help leaders and organizations overcome the obstacles, setbacks, and hurdles that prevent brilliant ideas and initiatives from reaching their full potential—to get "unstuck". Her five-step strategy of Envision—Expand—Build—Engage—Activate is at the same time brilliant in its simplicity *and* eminently actionable.

It allows leaders to drive momentum and attract resources to create widespread support along the full "conversion" journey, whether the need is a broader growth mindset, an openness to new business models requiring new internal activity systems and operating models, agility to pivot when necessary, investment in and establishment of innovation ecosystems, or creating a "love of learning" culture.

I'll be leveraging the book across my efforts as I help executives generate more new value. My advice to these leaders will be to buy *From Stuck to Scale* and use it with your organization to establish a flywheel of growth, as Andrea herself coins it so powerfully.

INTRODUCTION

THIS BOOK BEGAN when I lost a twenty-dollar bet.

It was a freezing cold day in Rochester, Minnesota, and we were just ending a twenty-week sprint designed to bring early-stage ideas all the way through to commercialization. There were sixteen teams with inspiring ideas that ranged from medical technologies to digital health solutions to devices geared to help people live healthier lives. Every team had been equipped with traditional tools, including strategic frameworks, competitive analysis, design thinking, customer discovery, lean startup, agile sprint frameworks, and economic analysis spreadsheets.

My role was to work with the leadership team to guide the process and accelerate success—new lines of business, fresh solutions to hairy problems, and business models that would drive long-term customer traction.

Months earlier, just before the first formal gathering to jumpstart the project, I had confidently placed a crisp twenty-dollar bill on the table with my bets on which teams would come out on top and which initiatives would die an early death. Positive that I could recognize winners, I factored in the elements that seemed to lead to innovation that got all the way across the finish line at scale. At the time, my evaluation of what it would take to lead the pack was largely formed by my impressions of how motivated the team was based on a strong elevator pitch, and how strong the underlying business model seemed to be based on written proposals. Where there was an innovative technology being proposed—like the use of AI, visual imaging, or tracking technologies—I factored in an analysis of the readiness level of the underlying technology.

The clincher was that a team worth betting twenty dollars on would have to meet my criteria for the strength of the underlying customer value, the viability of the economics outlined in the proposal, and my assessment of whether the people had the talent, fortitude, and grit to push innovation through the hurdles they'd face along the way.

During the next four months, we put the innovators and inventors through their paces. Everyone had to refine their vision multiple times, test and learn with multiple experiments, and aggressively pursue alternate avenues when their initial concepts didn't pan out.

The experience was *energizing* when an invention hit a win with the targeted customers; humbling when experts were faced with a wall of resistance—like when they couldn't land on an economic model that made sense; and *demoralizing* when leaders had to kiss goodbye fantastic technological ideas that never found a way to market.

At the beginning of the sprint, I was certain that I could predict which teams would advance beyond the others.

Sadly, the end of the sprint felt like a punch in the gut. I lost my twenty-dollar bet, and realized that the basic assumptions about building a compelling concept into a thriving business were wrong. The best initial ideas didn't make it to the end; the strongest technologies weren't enough to save some of the teams, and fantastic underdogs raced forward (to my surprise).

I wondered why I had been so blindsided, and how to improve the odds for success for *all* of the teams the next time. Why don't the best ideas become the best businesses? Why are there important projects that die, unnecessarily, on the vine?

As I stared at that twenty-dollar bill, I froze—struck by a strong sensation that this bet represented more than a wager on a one-time inability to pick winners. In the instant it took to hand over the money and admit defeat, I reflected on all the times when progress stalled—whether it was working with talented leaders, high-performing teams, or groundbreaking technologies—with no clear process for what to do next.

What I learned by working closely with those sixteen teams (and reflecting on the other 13,000 teams that shared their own sprints on the software platform I led) was the key to why important initiatives fail. I was determined to fix it.

Have you ever been there? Months into a project, and suddenly everything slows down, goes into endless loops, or worse, screeches to a halt?

Have you ever wondered why the things that help you start a project stop working? Have you tried more of the same, only harder, faster, louder, but still hit a wall? It doesn't have to be that way.

When it comes to the gnarliest parts of the struggle to overcome barriers and rethink options, teams are left without tools to guide them. Initiatives get stuck for different reasons at every stage of the commercialization process. Still, we have no formalized tools to get them unstuck. In the early stages of transforming an idea from an elevator pitch into a viable business, we typically tell leaders to pivot and find a novel business model. Where we miss the mark is that we never tell them the fundamentals of where to look for Plan B. Even worse, when it's time to guide their experiments and pilots toward escape velocity—viable and large-scale lines of business—we haven't taught them how to gain full support from suppliers, partners, internal champions, and, ultimately, long-term and loyal customers.

The traditional emphasis on ideas, prototypes, experiments, and standard competitive analysis doesn't address the hidden undertow that drags important ideas backward. In essence, we get stuck.

Our lack of focus on how to get unstuck leads to a sadly depressing result: we inadvertently give birth to orphans—projects without sufficient traction to nurture early-stage commercial initiatives toward their full potential.

Rochester's sixteen teams represented the very best levels of talent and technology with so much to offer. However, our inability to help them get unstuck left a considerable gap between them and customers who needed those products, technologies, and services. It was a lose-lose to which we can all relate.

What had gone wrong? What did we miss because we were limited by a traditional approach to strategy and innovation? What does it really take to get great ideas unstuck at each stage of development? How can we eliminate orphans and teach different skills to cohorts, teams, innovators, inventors, changemakers, and business leaders who want to drive growth and impact?

Over the five years that followed, I tested and refined a fresh set of tools that reverse the downward spiral that sets in when a project is midstream and can't find its footing—tools that focus not only on building great concepts, but also on engineering support and lasting commitment inside your organization and outside your company.

A month after I lost the twenty-dollar bet, I committed to meeting people who were experiencing the frustration of challenging market forces with no clear path forward. Little did I realize I accidentally encountered the perfect test case: Intergráficas, the largest compact disc manufacturer in Latin America. Intergráficas' issues were so universal that I've illustrated their case progress throughout the five stages outlined in this book.

There's a broader application I discovered about getting unstuck that calls for us to equip new tools right away: we must learn how to drive impact at scale. Whether we're leading initiatives in healthcare, circularity, AI, product development, manufacturing, community-based programs, or fintech, the only way to achieve success is to empower bigger ecosystems.

The talents that have served us well for the past decade—five-year plans, competitive analysis, incremental product improvement—aren't designed for today's world. We must swap out our tool kit to navigate challenges collaboratively and continue to build momentum without getting stalled.

I set out to solve the challenges of "stuck" for anyone who hits a wall.

It turns out that you
can bring ideas that
matter to tons of
people. But not the way
we were taught to do it.

5 STEPS
ENVISION, EXPAND, BUILD, ENGAGE, ACTIVATE

THIS HANDS-ON PLAYBOOK provides a set of tools designed to address the challenges of making innovation work. It's painful to have great technology with tremendous potential for impact that never reaches its fullest potential. It's challenging to envision a fantastic solution to a big problem that never gets across the finish line. It's also unfair to expect busy leaders with a lot on their plates to add an innovation initiative to their priority list. It's up to us to build support inside and outside our organizations to eliminate orphan projects.

You'll be pleased to know the solution comes down to five steps: Envision, Expand, Build, Engage, and Activate. Over the months after I lost my twenty dollars, I figured out the elements of "stuck" and solved the challenge of scale, working with teams in multiple sectors and geographies.

The *From Stuck to Scale* discipline worked with projects as diverse as an automotive company tackling cybersecurity in the US and China, to a Nordic wind company and a Canadian healthcare non-profit.

To reinforce and refine the model, I conducted research with leaders whose growth strategies are perfect illustrations of the *From Stuck to Scale* principles: Rappi, a Latin American omnichannel platform that started as a sandwich delivery service; Copenhagen Fintech, a mighty ecosystem backbone for fintech innovation; Mayo Clinic, a global healthcare giant; Hilti, a leader in B2B software and services; and Shimizu, a Japanese construction company with a vision beyond traditional construction.

Those experiences and conversations set the stage for this book, which codifies the steps we can all take to help our teams overcome obstacles and gain traction for important initiatives.

Envision

In the Envision stage, you will learn how to clarify and express the essence of your next initiative using four foundational tools to help grow your vision.

Through these tools, you will learn how to break down the walls keeping you and your team from innovation, envision a clear future for your goals, reimagine your company's innovation ecosystem, and take bold steps to action your initiatives.

The Envision toolkit includes four exercises:

1 Taking Stock
2 Now/Next
3 Sketch Your Idea
4 Four Quadrants

Expand

This next step will teach you how to apply technology, cross-industry opportunities, and different business models to make your next initiative bolder. Through the tools in this chapter, you will learn how to open your mind, stretch your thinking, consider emerging science, and nail down the burning questions that will make a difference in the success of your goals.

The five tools in the Expand step include:

1 The 4-Beat Story
2 Expanding the 4-Beat Story
3 Innovation Enablers
4 Opportunity Aperture
5 Ideaboard

Build

The third step of the system, Build, will show you how to make your initiative real, learn from errors, shift gears, modify your goals, and debug any potential problems. This chapter is about putting a stake in the ground, dynamically designing your initiative to accelerate learning, grow quickly, and tackle challenges head-on.

Five canvases in the Build toolbox will help you achieve the skills in this chapter:

1 Ideaboard (Part 2)
2 Experiment Tracker
3 Untapped Opportunities
4 Scale Optimizer Checklist
5 Bias and Blind Spot Tracker

Engage

This step is about bringing others into the fold. Your goal for this stage in the *From Stuck to Scale* system is to create maximum-value ecosystems.

Through the tools presented, you will determine your core principles to inspire others, change your thinking for maximum engagement from internal and external stakeholders, and build the perfect ecosystem to reach your goals.

Four tools in this chapter will help you understand and fulfill the Engage step:

1 Commitment Narratives
2 Impact Multiplier
3 Ecosystem Mapper
4 Transformative Leadership

I invite you to master the frameworks in the book to be inspired by stories of people like you who have succeeded in jumpstarting change and getting people on board using these five steps.

Activate

Finally, the Activate stage will teach you to enlist commitment and operationalize your initiative to ensure it thrives. You will learn about the core concepts of business activation, the dynamics behind action, how to become unstuck when you hit a real snag in your progress, and how to keep your initiative relevant in today's culture of perpetual refresh.

In this stage, we will look at four concluding tools that will get you unstuck:

1 The 4-Beat Activation Story
2 The 4-Quadrant Activation Plan
3 Activation Imperatives
4 Culture of Activation

How to use this workbook

From Stuck to Scale is designed as a program to bring early-stage initiatives to full activation and get you on the right track when you feel paralyzed by challenges. Each module is designed as a self-contained program that you can use to focus on one aspect of the process.

However, as a progressive system, each component builds on the prior ones to drive commitment and alignment from the people involved and to build scale and impact into the final result.

You might also want more guidance as you read and work through this book. You can find additional resources at www.andreakates.com, as well as at the end of the book.

And, if you'd like to do a quick check to pinpoint where you're stuck at this moment, you can take our three-minute Where Are You Stuck Diagnostic at www.andreakates.com/diagnostic.

Remember that most initiatives never reach success in silos. You'll learn more about this later, but the key to getting the most out of this book is working with your partners, colleagues, and teammates to collaborate on tools for maximum results. Share these worksheets with others to leverage their perspectives and develop your initiative to its fullest potential.

Before diving into the *From Stuck to Scale* process, we encourage you to explore your readiness for the journey ahead and pinpoint the place where you're most stuck today by taking the *From Stuck to Scale* Assessment.

TOOL: FROM STUCK TO SCALE ASSESSMENT

Purpose

How ready are you to go *From Stuck to Scale*? What will it take for you, your team, your organization and your community of customers, collaborators, constituents, and investors to align around what's possible, what's important, and which priorities should set your future direction?

The *From Stuck to Scale* Assessment is a perfect place to take stock of your current perspective, compare it to the perspectives of people around you, and chart a path toward next-level growth and impact.

Take the assessment yourself, and share it with your team members, people inside your organization, or your broader ecosystem.[1]
Once you've completed the *From Stuck to Scale* Assessment, it's time to Envision a fresh path to growth.

How to use it + example

This worksheet is an initial pulse check to pinpoint where in the process you're experiencing the greatest friction or frustration. It's also designed to be used as a comparative measure to see how your perceptions align with the perceptions of other people in your organization, your team, and your ecosystem.

Use the *From Stuck to Scale* Assessment as a rapid indicator to guide an intervention strategy and help you identify where to get started.

---

1   You can find a printable copy of the *From Stuck to Scale* Assessment to use with your colleagues or team on my website at www.andreakates.com.

Fill out the individual column with your assessment of your own readiness levels

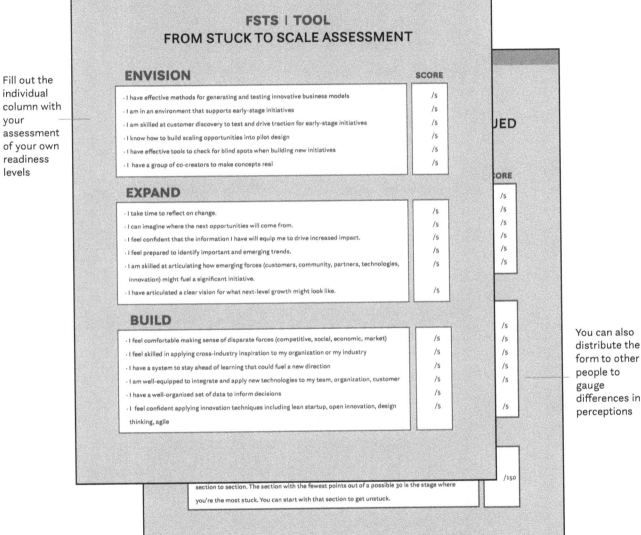

FSTS | TOOL
FROM STUCK TO SCALE ASSESSMENT

ENVISION

	SCORE
· I have effective methods for generating and testing innovative business models	/5
· I am in an environment that supports early-stage initiatives	/5
· I am skilled at customer discovery to test and drive traction for early-stage initiatives	/5
· I know how to build scaling opportunities into pilot design	/5
· I have effective tools to check for blind spots when building new initiatives	/5
· I have a group of co-creators to make concepts real	/5

EXPAND

	SCORE
· I take time to reflect on change.	/5
· I can imagine where the next opportunities will come from.	/5
· I feel confident that the information I have will equip me to drive increased impact.	/5
· I feel prepared to identify important and emerging trends.	/5
· I am skilled at articulating how emerging forces (customers, community, partners, technologies, innovation) might fuel a significant initiative.	/5
· I have articulated a clear vision for what next-level growth might look like.	/5

BUILD

	SCORE
· I feel comfortable making sense of disparate forces (competitive, social, economic, market)	/5
· I feel skilled in applying cross-industry inspiration to my organization or my industry	/5
· I have a system to stay ahead of learning that could fuel a new direction	/5
· I am well-equipped to integrate and apply new technologies to my team, organization, customer	/5
· I have a well-organized set of data to inform decisions	/5
· I feel confident applying innovation techniques including lean startup, open innovation, design thinking, agile	/5

section to section. The section with the fewest points out of a possible 30 is the stage where you're the most stuck. You can start with that section to get unstuck.

/150

You can also distribute the form to other people to gauge differences in perceptions

FSTS | TOOL
FROM STUCK TO SCALE ASSESSMENT

ENVISION

	SCORE
· I have effective methods for generating and testing innovative business models	/5
· I am in an environment that supports early-stage initiatives	/5
· I am skilled at customer discovery to test and drive traction for early-stage initiatives	/5
· I know how to build scaling opportunities into pilot design	/5
· I have effective tools to check for blind spots when building new initiatives	/5
· I have a group of co-creators to make concepts real	/5

EXPAND

	SCORE
· I take time to reflect on change	/5
· I can imagine where the next opportunities will come from	/5
· I feel confident that the information I have will equip me to drive increased impact	/5
· I feel prepared to identify important and emerging trends	/5
· I am skilled at articulating how emerging forces (customers, community, partners, technologies, innovation) might fuel a significant initiative	/5
· I have articulated a clear vision for what next-level growth might look like	/5

BUILD

	SCORE
· I feel comfortable making sense of disparate forces (competitive, social, economic, market)	/5
· I feel skilled in applying cross-industry inspiration to my organization or my industry	/5
· I have a system to stay ahead of learning that could fuel a new direction	/5
· I am well-equipped to integrate and apply new technologies to my team, organization, customer	/5
· I have a well-organized set of data to inform decisions	/5
· I feel confident applying innovation techniques including lean startup, open innovation, design thinking, agile	/5

ENGAGE

	SCORE
· I can clearly state the Why for a new project in formats that resonate with critical supporters	/5
· I have a strong plan for scaling innovation within the organization	/5
· I have a strong plan for scaling innovation within the ecosystem	/5
· I have strong support from key doers who will make a new initiative top priority	/5
· I have an infrastructure of tools and processes to accelerate progress	/5
· I am 100% prepared to stay ahead of future change	/5

ACTIVATE

· I am well-equipped in engaging individuals whose perspective is focused on:	
- Customer and stakeholder value drivers	/5
- Future-focused opportunities	/5
- Logistics	/5
- Technical and analytical applications	/5
· I have led consistent growth (revenue, customer base, user engagement, sales, partners) for the past 12 months	/5
· I am highly skilled at articulating the value of a new initiative for a broad spectrum of audiences	/5

FINAL SCORE

Add up the points in each section (Envision, Expand, Build, Engage, Activate). Each section has a top potential score of 30 points (5 points for each of 6 questions). Compare the subtotals from section to section. The section with the fewest points out of a possible 30 is the stage where you're the most stuck. You can start with that section to get unstuck.	/150

We don't need
to hit the wall.

To overcome
obstacles,
we need new
tools.

And a shift
in mindset.

STEP 1

ENVISION
SEEING THE FUTURE TODAY

GOAL: To clarify and express
the essence of your next initiative

WHERE MIGHT YOU BE STUCK?

In this chapter, we'll address some of the following Stuck Points—friction, resistance, obstacles, and challenges—that might sound like this:

- "It's difficult to articulate today's challenges in a crisp, clear framework."

- "The team is caught in the weeds or losing focus."

- "We're too limited in our thinking."

- "We're thinking too big and can't get practical."

- "We're thinking too practically and can't stretch our imaginations."

Unsure where your situation fits in?

Visit www.andreakates.com/diagnostic and take the Where Are You Stuck Diagnostic to take stock.

A team, a line of business, or a company is stuck and needs to find its next opportunity. They must land on the right breed of innovation that stretches their imaginations and challenges their assumptions. And they need specific tools to overcome different types of challenges at every step of the process.

T**HE RED STOP** light was about to change to walk. It was the end of a long conference, and I looked forward to some downtime to reflect. The restaurant across the street would be a great place to sit down with my journal, synthesize my notes, and send follow-ups on conversations.

Right before I was about to cross the street, a stranger next to me caught my attention.

"What do you do?" he asked me.

"I help people get their companies unstuck. What about you?"

"I run a company that's probably in the worst possible situation," he replied.

"I doubt it. Tell me more."

"Well," he said, "we own a compact disc (CD) music production company."

This was 2016, and Intergráficas was the leading CD manufacturer in Latin America, trying to deal with the reality that their industry was dying. By then, they had tried all the conventional approaches to redirect the organization's fate: process efficiency, design thinking, theory of constraints, lean startup, and strength, weakness, opportunities and threats (SWOT) analysis. But none of those methods could stop the death spiral and propel Intergráficas toward profitability.

"You might be right," I said. "That is the worst possible situation."

In the sixty seconds it took to cross the street, I agreed to hear him out and consider if there was anything that could reverse the trend. Doubling down on efficiency would never get to the crux of his problem, but blue-sky thinking was probably too outlandish to work. Here was a company with employees whose jobs would fade if this stranger—named Nicolas—couldn't figure it out.

I told Nicolas I couldn't promise there would be a way out, but I'd been piecing together tools and techniques that were designed to address his

> "One day I realized, oh, no—
> we're the walking dead."
>
> **NICOLAS CORTÁZAR,**
> Director, Intergráficas

exact situation—a situation that thousands of people were facing every day:

A team, a line of business, or a company is stuck and needs to find its next opportunity. They must land on the right breed of innovation that stretches their imaginations and challenges their assumptions. And they need specific techniques for overcoming different challenges at every step of the process.

As you'll read in this book, that afternoon, I sat down with Nicolas and charted out a game plan. Over the next year, we tested my tools with Nicolas' company. We started with three steps to challenge the status quo and create tangible experiments we could test in the market: Envision, Expand, and Build. To truly overcome the challenge of scale, we focused on Engage and Activate: engaging a core group that was truly committed to the new direction beyond CDs, and activating a large, extended community and interconnected ecosystem of customers, suppliers, and other people outside of the CD world.

In this chapter, Envision, you'll see how the process began. In subsequent chapters, you'll learn how Intergráficas navigated the path *From Stuck to Scale*.

By the time the story ends, by following the *From Stuck to Scale* playbook, they successfully discovered their path toward sustainable growth and achieved eight times revenue.

It wasn't a smooth ride.

You'll also learn how Intergráficas addressed moments of doubt, frustration, and near-bankruptcy. You'll hear how Nicolas dealt with resistance from all sides: investors, employees, customers, and even his own version of "Dr. No." You'll also have an insider's view into the crises and cliffhangers that emerged over five years of transformation. For example, when the company seemed to be getting a break, the COVID-19 pandemic appeared, challenging their new non-CD business model and cutting off the supply chain that was the lifeline to success.

INTERGRÁFICAS' STORY is the throughline of *From Stuck to Scale*. The progression of their narrative and my experimentation with strategies to help them find traction set the stage for the skills and tools in each section of the book.

To make sure you have the examples you need to get started toward your next level of impact, every chapter has an additional case study from a different industry: manufacturing, healthcare, fintech, an artificial intelligence startup, construction, technology, and a purpose-driven ecosystem leader that led an inspiring one-million-person co-creation initiative.

The universal, practical lessons of strategy, imagination, overcoming bad luck, and building on the good luck brought by twists of fate are designed to be a practical playbook to help you diagnose where you are today, expand your thinking about how to radically improve your impact, determine where you are stuck, and build on your desire to get unstuck toward game-changing success.

In a world begging us to go faster, we must resist the urge to speed forward and instead bring wisdom to the game.

This chapter serves as a compass for that wisdom, guiding you through the process of turning your innovative ideas into actionable strategies that lead to meaningful impact.

That's how we get *From Stuck to Scale*.

At the core of our journey is a five-step process. This chapter delves into the first of these steps: Envision. This foundational stage sets the tone for what follows, and within it we focus on four essential tools.

To maximize the effectiveness of the Envision process, we advocate a blend of individual reflection and collaborative teamwork. You will progress from conceptualization to a clear, actionable plan, considering internal transformations, customer-facing concepts, new business lines, innovative models, or ecosystem engagements. The journey begins with clarification.

Our ideas matter. In this module, Envision, we'll learn how to refine and express our initial ideas.

> When the spark of awareness arrives, we have a choice: do something, or let it go.

Your practical toolkit

This workbook equips you with practical tools and canvases, each serving a specific purpose in the Envision process. We provide detailed instructions and real-world examples, making it accessible and actionable. As part of the Envision step, you'll be introduced to the following tools to help you imagine your next initiative.

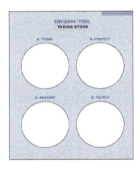

Taking Stock

A structured exercise to quickly sketch and summarize what's today, what perfect would look like, what's missing, and what you need to tackle.

Now/Next

Distills the Taking Stock snapshot. What are the core elements of your next initiative? Is it internal to your organization, or will it affect a larger ecosystem? What might the impact be?

Sketch Your Idea

Expresses the kernel of the initiative using simple stick figures and drawings. Applies the discipline of expressing your concept simply. Determines the first step you'll take toward activation.

Four Quadrants

Categorizes your strengths and surrounds your capabilities with other dimensions of the opportunity that can bring your initiative to life, build scale, and increase the impact.

CASE IN POINT
NICOLAS CORTÁZAR, DIRECTOR, INTERGRÁFICAS

It's cool to have the inside track on Shakira's musical career, show up at concerts to sell compact discs to fans, and stage events that promote Latin music. It's even cooler when you're the leading Colombian CD manufacturer and can ride the wave of Colombian talent like Shakira—who brought Grammy wins and global fame—to establish leadership as the CD company for musicians from all over Latin America. That was the position Intergráficas held in 2016.

They were at the top of a sexy field, which created an employee culture fueled by the buzz of the entertainment industry, a growing community of more than 7,000 musicians, and a rich ecosystem of agents, concert venues and studios, in addition to a huge base of customers who bought CDs and other merchandise.

The only problem: since its peak in the early 2000s, the compact industry had been driven into a nosedive by the popularity of online music. Intergráficas was holding on, but the writing was on the wall, and they desperately needed to find a new path. They were the walking dead.

What to do in a dying market?
Intergráficas DVD and CD sales 2007-2016 (million units)

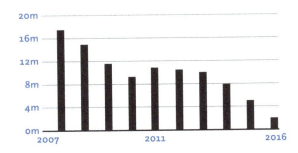

Source: Intergráficas

Nicolas asked himself the critical questions we can all relate to:

- **Improved efficiency**: How might we optimize our existing business model, apply the theory of constraints, and shift toward lean manufacturing to maximize efficiency?

- **New business model**: Will our future growth come from digging deeper inside our current industry?

- **Technology**: Can we find a new technology that might drive growth?

- **Emerging customer needs**: Is there a customer need that we can serve using our existing company strengths?

- **New industry**: How might we reconfigure our existing capabilities to gain traction in an industry outside of music?

As he envisioned a possible future for Intergráficas, he knew he had to consider multiple paths.

The Envision tools—Taking Stock, Now/Next, Sketch Your Idea, and Four Quadrants—became the core of the company's articulation of hunches for the future. They used these foundational frameworks to define potential areas for growth.

To innovate, first we need to take stock of the walls in our company that are inhibiting change.

TOOL: TAKING STOCK

 ## Purpose

As we picture our next direction, we have shifted from thinking about growth to putting initial ideas down on paper. This tool helps us describe the basics: where we stand today, where we'd like to be, and our perspectives on what's missing from our current equation (in other words, our walls). It provides guidelines for a new initiative.

We can also think of "perfect" from the perspective of our future state, working backward and asking, "Where might we be positioned to make a difference?"

We can be motivated by several factors: The emergence of new technologies, awareness of a new customer need, desire to integrate new market data, societal shifts, and the emergence of new players (startups, large companies, researchers, people in our extended ecosystem).

 ## How to use it + example

Do this first as an individual, and then share it with your team or group to open the discussion on where to focus next. Focus on and summarize what's happening today, what perfect would look like, what's missing, and what you want to/need to tackle (see the suggestions in each circle).

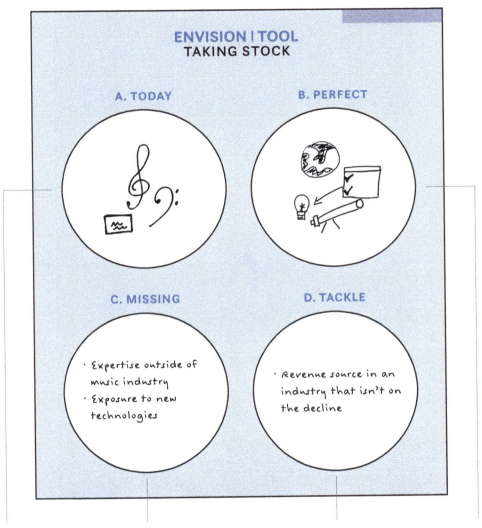

ENVISION | TOOL
TAKING STOCK

A. TODAY

B. PERFECT

C. MISSING

· Expertise outside of music industry
· Exposure to new technologies

D. TACKLE

· Revenue source in an industry that isn't on the decline

Visual represen-
tation of current
perception, role,
and transactional
strengths of
the team

Listing of the
desired state
(without the
requirement
to know how
to get there

Specific actions to
take, enhanced
capacity and capabil-
ities to master, and
discovery process
steps to begin

Sketch of the desire to
move beyond transactions
and compliance and
become more central to
the company's strategic
leadership

Your turn: Instructions

Fill in the sections on the opposite page
as follows:

- **TODAY.** Sketch where you are today, within
  the context of the area where you'd like to
  increase your team's or your organization's
  impact.

- **PERFECT.** Sketch some ideas about what an
  ideal future might look like in this arena.
  Where is there an unmet need? Where
  might you create impact?

- **MISSING.** Using short phrases, write down
  key concepts that describe what's missing
  from today that would take you closer to
  your envisioned future.

- **TACKLE.** Using short phrases, list a few areas
  you'd like to focus on to make progress.

ENVISION | TOOL
TAKING STOCK

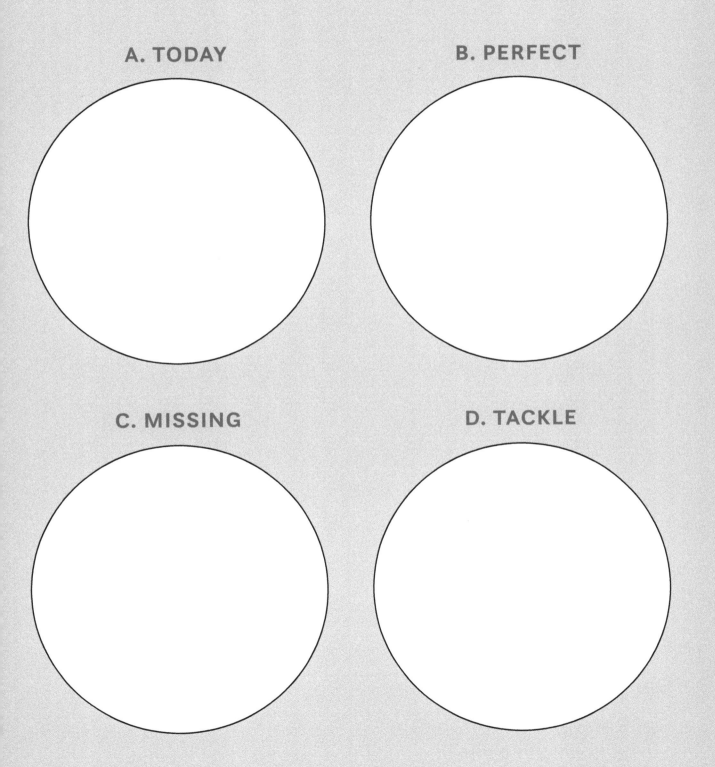

A. TODAY

B. PERFECT

C. MISSING

D. TACKLE

NOTES

Key takeaway

This process purposely encourages a combination of open, creative expression, sensemaking, and synthesis. Companies must actively identify, understand, and address the barriers to innovation, ranging from resistance to change and resource limitations to cultural constraints and unclear innovation strategies.

Organizations can pave the way for meaningful innovation and strategic growth in a rapidly evolving business landscape by taking stock of these obstacles and envisioning a future state.

What to do next

Synthesize your key findings from the Taking Stock tool into a group document using the Now/Next framework. Now that you know where your company is today, what your vision looks like, what you're missing and what you need to tackle, you can start making some bold steps toward change.

We present the Now/Next tool—a strategic instrument designed to distill insights from your initial Taking Stock exercise. This tool will serve as the compass by which you can discern the core elements of your next significant initiative.

TOOL: NOW/NEXT

 ## Purpose

Use this tool to integrate key ideas from the Taking Stock worksheet. Early-stage initiatives begin with a combination of insights about emerging opportunities, customer preference shifts, ecosystem changes, or new technologies. Summarize the essence of where you are now and your envisioned future state, without getting stuck in operational details or constraints.

 ## How to use it + example

Synthesize critical insights and information from Taking Stock into a composite of your next area. Do it individually, share with the group, and use the worksheet in a facilitated conversation to group common responses, discuss priorities, and refine the consideration set of future initiatives. Distill the possible directions into a short list of what "next" looks like. Apply initial filters to crystallize the key components of your concept.

Description of the organization's key resources, uniqueness, and internal processes, as well as potential limitations and opportunities for growth

ENVISION | TOOL
NOW / NEXT

A. NOW

Declining revenues

Mindset is not future focused

Identification with "sexy" industry

Employees with expertise in manufacturing

B. NEXT

Thriving, growing market

Employment future for employees

Double down on either music, technology, or another competency

Description of what the organization could be in an ideal future, without concern for how that future might be achieved

Your turn: Instructions

Fill in the sections on the opposite page
as follows:

- **NOW.** In the top section, jot down key
  phrases that describe your current situation. If you're doing the exercise as a team,
  everyone can do their version of "Now."

- **NEXT.** In the bottom section, write key
  phrases that describe your future state.
  Don't worry if you don't know how you'll get
  there. What is the ideal future for your organization or team? What are the elements
  and components of "Next?"

Reflect on all the elements and components.
Synthesize all the versions of "Next" from
everyone's canvases. Bring those forward into
the next step, where you'll sketch your idea.

ENVISION | TOOL
NOW / NEXT

A. NOW

B. NEXT

NOTES

Key takeaway

This model can be applied broadly, including to the leadership of internal initiatives, driving a line of business on a new path, spearheading a co-creation initiative, and even complex, multi-year innovation projects.

Organizations must recognize that it involves generating creative ideas and making strategic decisions to choose bold and impactful initiatives.

What to do next

Gather your thinking into a sketch using the Sketch Your Idea framework. When creativity is flowing, sometimes it can be hard to pin down the exact path toward the new world we're striving for. Sketching your ideas as pictures can help you to distill and clarify your thoughts and ideas.

TOOL: SKETCH YOUR IDEA

 Purpose

Use this worksheet to develop multiple per-spectives on the initiative. Reflect on how you'd get started.

 How to use it + example

Express the themes from the Now/Next document as a specific initiative (a drawing) and articulate (in words) the first step you'd envision as part of your activation plan. What will it take to make significant progress? Combining both big-picture thinking as well as action steps sets the course for imagination as well as implementation.

Visual representation of ideas in starting form, including innovative processes, products, and potential hurdles to overcome

ENVISION | TOOL
SKETCH YOUR IDEA

A. YOUR IDEA SKETCH

B. FIRST STEP

Meet with 3D printers

Actionable steps that strip apart the big ideas into smaller and more executable parts

Your turn: Instructions

Fill in the sections on the opposite page as follows:

- **YOUR IDEA SKETCH.** Synthesize the themes from the Now/Next tool into a concrete initiative that could be driven by your team or your organization. What might be a go-to-market idea, product, service, or challenge that could have a high impact on your customers or your market? Sketch the elements that represent the main components of the initiative.

- **FIRST STEP.** Write down the first step you'd take to make your vision a reality

TEAM INTEGRATION. If you're working with a team to complete the Sketch Your Idea tool, facilitate a session to integrate everyone's sketches into one master sketch. Teams can compare their answers to refine their thinking about the initiative to tackle.

ENVISION | TOOL
SKETCH YOUR IDEA

A. YOUR IDEA SKETCH

B. FIRST STEP

NOTES

Key takeaway

The process of sketching helps you tap into your imagination. The first-step component of this practice balances creativity with practical thinking about how to make the future sketch real.

What to do next

To prepare for the progression of your work, you'll copy the sketch into the Four Quadrants tool. You'll also categorize your answer to question two: What's the first step you'd take to activate your vision? You'll be introduced to four distinct quadrants, and you will copy your answer from Sketch Your Idea into the corresponding quadrant on the Four Quadrant form.

TOOL: FOUR QUADRANTS

 ### Purpose

This exercise begins by approaching a new initiative or novel direction with a distinctive set of values and skills that plant early seeds to gain widespread support in the future.

It takes a combination of Engagement, Broader Thinking, Logistics, and Data and Tech to bring the best concepts forward and operationalize them with maximum impact.

 ### How to use it + example

Begin by transferring the first step from Sketch Your Idea to the quadrant where it fits best (in this case, "Meet with 3D printers" fits in the Engagement quadrant).

Jot down your activation perspective from Sketch Your Idea in the quadrant where it fits best. Examples of the types of sketches you might work on could be an innovative product or service design, an internal transformation within your own company, an ecosystem strategy, or a collaboration designed to bring a co-creation opportunity to market.

Establishment of steps to engage key stakeholders within the organization and a broader ecosystem

ENVISION | TOOL
FOUR QUADRANTS

A. ENGAGEMENT

- Meet with 3D printers
- Conversations with current employees
- Meetings with music community: platforms, festivals, artists

B. BROADER THINKING

- Imagine what we might do with KFC
- Picture the 3D healthcare arena

High-level analysis on potential for expansion and growth

YOUR SKETCH

C. LOGISTICS

- Deep dive into our current production six sigma processes

D. DATA + TECH

- Explore 3D printing as new tech platform

Articulation of opportunities to think innovatively about key processes

Description of relevant research and new technologies that could accelerate progress

Your turn: Instructions

Start by copying your sketch from the Sketch Your Idea tool into the square at the center of the opposite page.

Next, fill in the remaining sections as follows:

- **ENGAGEMENT.** Who would you need to connect with to bring this initiative forward?

- **BROADER THINKING.** How might you make your initial sketch even bolder?

- **LOGISTICS.** How might you think more innovatively about operations and processes to move faster or to have a greater impact?

- **DATA + TECH.** How might you apply new technologies, platforms, and other research insights?

ENVISION | TOOL
FOUR QUADRANTS

A. ENGAGEMENT

B. BROADER THINKING

YOUR SKETCH

C. LOGISTICS

D. DATA + TECH

NOTES

Key takeaway

Too often, innovation is seen as an exercise that keeps people in silos. Sticky-note ideation sessions don't include the compliance team. Technical sessions don't include customer-facing teams. The entire innovation process must include people, expertise, resources, buy-in, insights, and in-depth perspectives representing all four quadrants to activate transformation.

What to do next

Work with other people on your team to fill in additional steps you'd take to bring your initiative forward. At the end of the exercise, you'll have articulated your next vision with components from every quadrant required to activate a new idea.

SPOTLIGHT STORY: SHIMIZU
A Fresh Approach

How a 220-year-old company is innovating innovation with a Choukensetsu (Construction++) mindset

I remember standing at the doorway of the corporate innovation center in Silicon Valley and thinking, *no one is innovating this way*. The wall in front of me had a display with detailed descriptions of emerging technologies, ranging from 3D imaging to advanced mobile applications. On the wall to the right was a collection of standing foam core boards covered with sticky notes expressing customer insights, grouped thematically. To the left were project canvases inspired by key advisers: Ikujiro Nonaka, a legendary thought leader in knowledge creation in organizations; Barry Katz, a pioneer with IDEO in design thinking; Steve Blank, originator of the customer development method that led the lean startup movement; and Henry Chesbrough, originator of the discipline of open innovation. When I turned around to the back wall, I saw a long list of societal challenges that included loneliness, aging population and disaster recovery.

Immediately, I could sense that there was a visionary leader at work—someone who could build corporate strategy on a framework of advanced technologies and creativity as well as societal issues, all rooted in a cohesive philosophy. I was about to meet him for the first time.

Sitting at the table in the middle of the room was Mohi Ahmed, the person in charge of the Center. He explained his deeply held values about how a company might define its future initiatives by integrating what's known, what's emerging, what's important to today's customers, and—a component of strategy that took me by surprise—what's important to society.

Accustomed to walking into rooms like these and being confronted with either a SWOT diagram to display tomorrow's challenges through the lens of today's products, customers, and competitors, or a room of creative ideas as the two extremes of strategic innovation, I found Mohi's "four-wall" approach to be a refreshing alternative and a powerful way to guide the first step in the *From Stuck to Scale* process: Envision.

In the years that followed, I worked collaboratively with Mohi in Silicon Valley, hosting visiting teams trying to bring early-stage ideas through to commercial fruition and traveling to Asia to equip innovators with the skills to innovate. Through the projects we worked on together, I came to appreciate Mohi's depth of vision and experienced firsthand the potential unleashed when a large organization weaves together business acumen, creativity, societal impact, and a capacity to co-create on a broad scale.

Since the time of our collaborations in Silicon Valley, Mohi moved to Japan to work with Shimizu, the company where he started his professional career when he was in his early twenties. Today, Mohi is working closely with the senior management team focused on building innovation capacity for Shimizu's workforce and bringing extended innovation capabilities to Shimizu's customers and partners, as well as to an ecosystem of collaborators and beneficiaries.

Shimizu combines 220 years of heritage with a fresh perspective on the future

Since 1804, Shimizu has been responsible for landmark construction projects in Japan and beyond. The company's projects include award-winning office buildings, university campuses, hospitals, airport terminals, technology facilities, tunnels, bridges and sports stadiums.

Two hundred and twenty years after their founding, Shimizu is on the brink of a new era that marries its heritage with an expansive vision for "smart innovation" using a mindset known as *Choukensetsu* (Construction++), which the company president describes as the critical components for the company's growth. As Shimizu's Executive Officer and Executive Innovator, Mohi Ahmed is charged with bringing smart innovation to life. Mohi is currently working very closely with the president, the senior management team, and other leaders across Shimizu's ecosystem to apply the combined forces of corporate innovation, societal impact and technology. Ultimately, smart innovation and the *Choukensetsu* mindset will enable Shimizu to extend beyond traditional construction with the ambition of enabling society to become more resilient, inclusive and sustainable.

For Shimizu, the next wave of business growth starts with *Choukensetsu* (Construction++) mindset

Shimizu's president, Kazuyuki Inoue, originated the concept of *Choukensetsu* (Construction++) to describe an expansive mindset that will prepare the organization for company-wide transformation by applying an integrated process. The team articulates *Choukensetsu* as Construction++. The first plus symbolizes a commitment to nurturing relationships with others inside and outside the company. The second plus describes a dynamic where Shimizu will grow in concert with both their customers as well as society. The term "Construction" is not limited only to construction; rather it could be core, adjacent, and even new areas of business as a means to society's goal of those of the company's customer. *Choukensetsu* as a business philosophy communicates Shimizu's vision to surround construction with two compelling forces: co-creation outside the company's walls, and the anticipation of societal needs beyond physical buildings.

In 2022, Shimizu established the Business Innovation Unit (BIU), now led by Mohi Ahmed, reporting directly to Shimizu President, Kazuyuki Inoue, to lead a company-wide transformation based on *Choukensetsu* mindset that builds on Shimizu's Credo (The Analects and the Abacus), Management Principles, Vision, and Shimizu Mind (Company's DNA), together with others inside and outside the company.

Choukensetsu (Construction++) poses refreshing questions to start the strategic innovation process

On day one, in many innovation labs and studios focused on construction, the opening question posed might be, "Who else needs an airport?" or "How might we bring world-class skills to build the next structure for our customers?"

There's nothing wrong with that approach. The set of solutions could include more sustainable building materials, AI-enabled design, and an array of inspiring ecosystem collaborations. But they'd all be anchored in physical structures and the technologies that could bring the design and build process to the next level.

Contrast the starting questions at Shimizu as part of their *Choukensetsu* (Construction++) mindset with a point of departure focused on society's basic needs:

- How might we create resilient communities outside of cities?

- How might we rethink disaster recovery to drive security?

- How might we reimagine reliable infrastructure that transcends buildings, to bring more flexible solutions for transportation, communication, and shared learning?

By starting with different questions, Shimizu can tackle big ideas in collaboration with their customers and global partners at universities, technology startups, governments, and corporations from different industries. *Choukensetsu* articulates the responsibility Shimizu believes they have to society—a responsibility that transcends traditional construction.

WeInnovate: a platform that enables everyone to envision and innovate

Mohi believes innovation is everyone's job, and is committed to engage all employees across the company in the innovation journey. To facilitate this company-wide movement, Shimizu's BIU introduced a platform they call WeInnovate. WeInnovate supports co-creation and integrates a unique, interconnected innovation process they designed called DDRS (D – Discover, D – Define, R – Refine, S – Scale). Through DDRS, teams take on projects to solve some of society's biggest problems: resilience, inclusivity, and sustainability.

Consistent with the *Choukensetsu* mindset, the discovery process doesn't start with questions about construction. Their Envision step starts by engaging customers, internal and external partners, thinkers, and practitioners from both Japan and beyond.

Shimizu's Fast and Wise standard for innovation brings the best of both worlds. The company can respond quickly to pressing challenges, but always with an eye toward broader implications and the future of society.

Shimizu's Smart Innovation Ecosystem: NOVARE represents a new breed of innovation campus

In 2023, Shimizu opened an innovation campus to bring its future vision to life. At the heart of Tokyo lies a 32,200-square-meter campus called NOVARE, a multi-facility complex. The name "NOVARE" is derived from the Latin word meaning "to make new." Shimizu chose NOVARE to be the core descriptor for their five-facility innovation campus, which houses core activities that will bring the company into the future and allow teams and partners to co-create with them:

NOVARE Hub: Gathering place for co-creation and open innovation

NOVARE Lab: Research facility for experimentation and emerging technologies

NOVARE Academy: Training center for in-person and virtual talent development

NOVARE Archives: Repository for resources and reference materials

Former Shibusawa Residence: NOVARE's envisioning of the future, which bridges to the company's roots

As a reminder of their heritage, Shimizu relocated the historic residence of Eiichi Shibusawa, one of the most prominent Japanese industrialists of the 1900s. It was built by Kisuke Shimizu II, and the original house now stands as a reminder of the thread of innovation that's been part of Shimizu's DNA for decades.

Ongoing experimentation led by the Business Innovation Unit (BIU) of Shimizu

Two years into the BIU's work, there are inspiring examples of missions they're driving to bring Shimizu into collaborations with a broad ecosystem of partners.

Here are some examples:

- **The Remote Island** model is an experiment to establish some model cases of resilient, inclusive, and sustainable islands in Japan and beyond.

  Significance: Japan is a nation of islands, but traditional construction companies would not proactively extend their reach to address the needs of small, remote islands.

- **The Small-Town** model focuses on revitalizing rural communities to address a dramatic nationwide loss of residents.

  Significance: As the younger generation moved to cities, the rural communities suffered. The generation of parents was separated from their children and grandchildren. Shimizu is exploring groundbreaking ways to revitalize small towns and help urban families feel connected with the senior generation.

- **Future Society Beyond 5G/6G** partners with major research institutions in Finland, Japan and beyond.

  Significance: Shimizu envisions 5G/6G telecommunications as more than simply a building specification on a checklist. Their bold vision addresses the human needs in the workplace and the home, even during major natural disasters.

As a foundational set of guiding principles, the *Choukensetsu* mindset roots Shimizu in rich relationships with the communities it serves, bringing a higher level of shared purpose in the blending of human needs, advanced technologies and human experiences that allow the company to dream bigger, envision the next century, and establish the foundation for a broad network of partners, communities and collaborators to innovate fast and wise. All these elements prepare Shimizu to create a new meaning for the concept of construction.

AT A GLANCE: SHIMIZU

TOPIC	Shimizu bridges its heritage to a bold future vision: tackle vexing challenges beyond traditional construction in collaboration with customers and communities. Ongoing experiments include the future of energy, natural disaster damage mitigation, and projects designed to create a resilient, inclusive and sustainable society.
FROM STUCK TO SCALE STEP	Envision
WHERE PEOPLE GET STUCK	Developing a culture of co-creation inside an architectural, engineering and construction-oriented organization. Thinking way beyond traditional construction.
HOW THE FROM STUCK TO SCALE APPROACH WORKED BETTER THAN TRADITIONAL STRATEGY	The Envision tools look deceptively simple, but they serve as a catalyst for a very different consideration set than tools like SWOT. The suite of tools forces leaders to shift from analytics to sketching, to push a team's ambitions beyond the constraints of today's strengths. Shimizu augmented their Envisioning with a Discover-Define-Refine-Scale (DDRS) process that encouraged leaders to look at their business landscape with fresh eyes.
BREAKTHROUGH MOMENT	Integrating partnerships to take on bold societal challenges. Establishing WeInnovate as the common platform and common language for innovation brings needs into the innovation discovery process right from the start.
IMPACT	Redefines the fundamentals of construction.
KEY INSIGHT	Don't assume that your company's best future will come from connecting the dots in a predictable way, which in Shimizu's case would have limited them to better and faster building construction.
HOW YOU CAN APPLY THIS	Resist the urge to edit your team's ambitions in the Envision stage. Remember that in the early stages of innovation, worrying about potential implementation challenges can suffocate creativity and unnecessarily limit future impact.

CHAPTER SUMMARY

>> Key insights

The first step in the *From Stuck to Scale* process is the Envision phase, where individuals and teams are encouraged to clarify and express the essence of their next initiative. This involves understanding the current state, envisioning the future, and determining necessary actions to bridge the gap.

>> Key Stuck Points

STUCK POINTS: FRICTION, RESISTANCE, OBSTACLES, CHALLENGES	TOOL TO USE	HOW IT WORKS
You're struggling to articulate today's challenges in a crisp, clear framework.	Taking Stock	Allows everyone to describe the current state of a project and the gaps they need to address. A litmus test to align the team and pinpoint challenges.
The team is caught in the weeds or losing focus.	Now/Next	Forces everyone to recommit to the end goals and the future state for your customers, your company and society.
You're too limited in your thinking.	Sketch Your Idea	The process of drawing forces different thinking than the process of developing spreadsheets or describing your idea with words or pitches. You'll unleash more creative connections through sketching.
You're thinking too big and can't get practical. OR You're thinking too practically and can't stretch your imaginations.	Four Quadrants	Each of us has habits in how we conceptualize the path toward growth. Sometimes we lean in on analytics to try to solve problems, calculate risk, apply systems thinking, and think operationally. Other times, we keep our thinking in the clouds without the bricks we need to build fundamental components. The discipline of forcing articulation from the perspectives of engaging others, and thinking of the big picture, helps with drilling down into operational possibilities.

>> Key actions

The key action in this chapter is to use the provided tools, such as Taking Stock, Now/Next, Sketch Your Idea, and Four Quadrants, to refine and express initial ideas for the next initiative. This includes sketching, summarizing, and categorizing to understand the initiative's core components clearly.

>> Key question

The key question to address in this chapter is:

"What is the essence of our next initiative, and how can we bridge the gap between the current state and the envisioned future?"

>> Commitment

The key commitment is to engage in the process of Envisioning the next initiative seriously and collaboratively, both individually and as a team. This includes filling out the provided canvases and using the tools provided to articulate a clear path forward for the initiative.

The gravest regret?

Letting fear of
execution stifle
your best ideas.

STEP 2

EXPAND
FINDING NEW HORIZONS

GOAL: Apply technology,
cross-industry opportunities,
and business models to go bolder

WHERE MIGHT YOU BE STUCK?

In this chapter, we'll address some of the following Stuck Points—friction, resistance, obstacles, and challenges—that may sound something like this:

- "We can't tell a clear story about the challenge we need to tackle."

- "We're caught in incrementalism."

- "New technologies and new business models seem overwhelming."

- "We're in a fixed mindset."

- "We don't know how to state our assumptions clearly enough to test them in the Build stage."

Unsure where your situation fits in?

Visit www.andreakates.com/diagnostic and take the *From Stuck to Scale* Diagnostic to take stock.

Intergráficas was at
the top of their game
as a CD producer by any
measure of traditional
benchmarking.

T**HE PROBLEM** was that producing music CDs was a dying game. Nicolas led the company through most of the strategy frameworks: SWOT, lean startup, Blue Ocean, the theory of constraints, design thinking, five forces. They had successfully optimized every process they could, making them a lean machine with no market and, therefore, no future.

Despite months spent searching for a new direction, nothing they did magically revealed a path out of their doom loop.

I flew to Bogotá to work with the team. They were enthusiastic as individuals, but justifiably disheartened.

How could it be that the industry that Intergráficas loved so much had left them in the cold by embracing music distribution models that excluded CDs? Was there any hope for the company to survive? Might there be some cache of coal inside their four walls that could be polished into a gem? Could they redirect their core competencies? Was there a technological innovation that might be applied (3D printing, for example)? Could their ecosystem partners help uncover a path to profitability?

During our first immersion session, we looked at the facts in every way we could. We realized that in the Expand phase, the most important tools had two aspects to them. First, everyone needed to explore opportunities to take what they knew how to do and reconfigure it to fit the future. We called that the "go-to."

But the toughest part of the Expand phase is the "give up" component to thinking bigger.

It was as if I could read everyone's minds: "What if the future we're imagining doesn't have a place for *me* in it?"

As Nicolas and I worked with the team, we were aware that *From Stuck to Scale* was not simply a theoretical process for a staff retreat. We were crafting the future of people whose livelihoods and identities were on the line.

We needed to create narratives that worked, articulate the truly make-or-break questions, and bravely commit to learning. To dig into fresh perspectives, we talked to people: investors, musicians, technologists, app developers, customers, and music festival producers. To stretch our imaginations, we sought out people from fields we needed to learn about: 3D printing experts, small business owners, corporate leaders from adjacent industries, and even trend experts.

The pressure was on. The company had to expand.

THE TOOLS in this chapter explain how Intergráficas expanded their range of options to escape the downward spiral of the CD manufacturing industry.

Have you ever faced that dreaded moment when your tried-and-true product no longer performs as it used to? Have you ever struggled to maintain profitability or raced to respond to a shift in your market?

Sometimes there's a dramatic event like a pandemic that sounds the alarm for change. Sometimes it's the allure of a bright, shiny object like AI or the future of work that signals the need for transformation. Other times it's a slow erosion of profits that forces us to take action.

What we rarely lack are ideas. Thanks to the last decade's advances in business tools, we have the capacity to generate ideas. Design thinking, open innovation, hackathons, sprints, labs, studios, accelerators, and incubators have created a torrent of ideas. Unfortunately, this abundance comes with a curse: as leaders, we're less confident than ever in navigating the path from nascent concepts to scalable opportunities.

We wonder where we should place our bets. We worry about the risks if we choose the wrong direction. We realize how ill-equipped we are to develop initiatives that are not simply incremental improvements on where we are today.

Step two in the five-step odyssey to get unstuck is Expand. It's specifically designed to mold the initial concepts we developed in the Envision stage into frameworks that can be tested in step three, Build.

Your practical toolkit

The Expand step teaches you to apply technology, cross-industry opportunities, and different business models to make your next initiative bolder, and provides you with five canvases designed to propel your next initiative forward.

In this chapter, we resist the urge to lean on traditional strategy tools. They were not created for today's world. Instead, Expand taps into insights from other industries, emerging technologies, and novel go-to-market options.

The 4-Beat Story

Summarizes the future and/or unmet need, the anticipated impact and success metrics.

Expanding the 4-Beat Story

Teaches you how to elevate your narrative to captivate your audience and stakeholders. This step involves gathering feedback from three perspectives: positive reinforcement, critical evaluation, and broader context.

Innovation Enablers

Identifies the tools and resources necessary for innovation to thrive.

All of the examples reflect the real-world journey that Intergráficas took from the doom cycle toward eight times revenue growth.

We get feedback from a wide range of people. We reach out for both critical feedback as well as expansive perspectives.

Through Expand, we land on the concepts we'll test in the Build phase.

Opportunity Aperture

Sharpens your focus on the most promising opportunities. This exercise will help you piece together components of best practices from organizations outside your industry to set the standard for your initiative.

Ideaboard

Frames each of your initiatives with a context to begin to test and learn in the Build stage.

CASE IN POINT
BUNMI AKINYEMIJU, PARTNER, GREENHOUSE CAPITAL AFRICA

What's the point of scaling a company, anyway? Hint: It's not growth for growth's sake.

Have you ever experienced a Eureka moment right in the middle of a casual morning coffee with someone—something so inspiring that you suddenly cleared your calendar to extend the conversation? That's what happened when I had my first meeting with Bunmi Akinyemiju. What started out as an informal exchange of ideas about entrepreneurship, technology, and the drivers of business success developed into a deeper discussion that highlighted critical questions we should ask ourselves before we launch into the Expand stage of the scaling process:

- What's the underlying reason for business growth?

- What does it take to prime early-stage companies for investment and get them ready to scale?

- Where will we hit the wall?

- Where might we push toward breakthroughs?

That morning, I learned a lot about Bunmi's views, informed by his work at both GreenHouse Capital Africa and Venture Garden Group, two organizations he co-founded and runs today. When I asked him about his end goal, he was clear: build economic agency for people living in Africa through job creation and the development of large-scale African companies.

My first cup of coffee with Bunmi not only provided enough caffeine to get me through the afternoon, but fueled a series of exchanges that helped me understand his more than two-decades-long track record as an entrepreneur, venture studio leader, investor, policy advisor, and ecosystem catalyst. To experience Green-House Capital and Venture Garden's work first-hand, I jumped on planes from California to multiple African countries for site visits across diverse parts of the continent.

After dozens of conversations, I came to appreciate how Bunmi and his team have rethought the building blocks for a growth economy. Through Bunmi's eyes, the components that frequently exist as silos—entrepreneurial talent, job creation, training, university collaboration, government, and the private sector—require special orchestration to create jobs for the millions of graduates coming out of African universities that outnumber the available positions in Africa today, and, ultimately, to build large, African-owned companies.

Bunmi started out as a teen entrepreneur

At age fifteen, Bunmi Akinyemiju figured out that his love of technology and his knack for commerce could create a steady revenue stream, and at age eighteen he co-founded his first company. Being a teen founder gave Bunmi an early start in learning what it took to go from zero to one: seeing a market need and figuring out how to serve customers with an important product, platform, or service. After launching three companies in Michigan, with one successful exit, he asked himself how he might apply what he'd learned to a bigger context: looking continent-wide at Africa, with a goal of incubating and growing technology companies. In 2011, he co-founded Venture Garden Group with a focus on startups created *in* Africa or *for* Africans.

In just over a decade, Venture Garden Group (VGG) and Greenhouse Capital (GHC) have had a transformative impact across technology, capital, and talent in Africa, focused on sectors that have the most transformative impact on emerging economies.

The diaspora also plays a critical role in providing talent, management expertise, and executive bench strength.

The entrepreneur plants a garden

Venture Garden Group is a venture holding company that incubates new ideas and turns them into companies. The team initially focused on creating startups with innovative solutions in industries that require data automation, infrastructure, and digital payments such as energy, aviation, agriculture, and education. One of their early portfolio companies, Edutech Global, took a novel look at training the talent required to empower the youth of Africa, considering the high demand for education—over one million applicants annually, without enough carrying capacity in the 126 universities.

Used with permission from GreenHouse Capital

GreenHouse Capital helps companies get through the valley of death: stalled growth

Bunmi and his team observed a pattern for early-stage companies that mirrored the "valley of death" faced by startups around the world, and they decided to address the problem head-on. Companies reached a certain level of revenue growth—sometimes with the assistance of grant funding or subsidies—but couldn't scale. They launched GreenHouse Capital as a corporate VC to use risk capital as a mechanism to get startups over the hump toward expansion. Their investment portfolio includes platforms in fintech and payments like Flutterwave and Pezesha and companies like BoxCommerce.

Collectively, GreenHouse's investment capital focuses on payments, lending, blockchain, eKYC, and ecommerce platforms for small business and corporates—businesses that are fundamental to economic transformation in African countries.

So far, Venture Garden Group has incubated more than twenty companies. GreenHouse Capital has invested in over sixty companies across Africa and the Middle East, creating one of the largest venture investment holding companies on the continent. As a venture holding company, Venture Garden Group builds some assets from scratch; other times, GreenHouse Capital identifies existing companies where capital investment will be the catalyst for expansion.

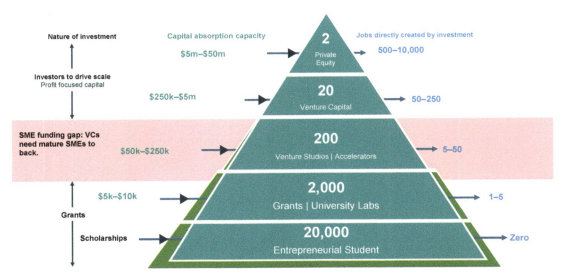

Early-stage initiatives won't automatically scale

"Today, there's a gap between grant/accelerator-funded entrepreneurs that succeed in the early stage, versus fully scalable enterprises. For us, the goal isn't to create 'grantpreneurs' or companies that excel at being able to go through accelerator programs like Y Combinator or Techstars but that ultimately lack capital absorption capacity. Scaling those early successes requires relationships with corporate partners (for market access) and universities (for talent) to transform thriving saplings into forests."

BUNMI AKINYEMIJU, Partner, Greenhouse Capital Africa

GreenHouse Capital funds companies that have capital absorption capacity—the ability to apply investment dollars toward significant operational growth in four areas:

1   Significant geographic expansion

2   Go-to-market strategies that drive strategic distribution

3   Governance capacity to support issues and complexities that come with significant growth (policy influence, board, and advisors)

4   Experienced technology and talent bench, including seasoned leaders from the African diaspora to accelerate progress

Growing an employment ecosystem means shifting gears

The "triple helix" of support driving early-stage success for the companies in GreenHouse Capital's portfolio included seed funds, innovation, and R&D support. But those same companies require a boost from a *different* triple helix of partners to push beyond the limits of organic growth and establish a thriving employment ecosystem:

1   Policy influence to pave the way for business and job creation

2   Corporations + small companies to foster alliances that bring mutual benefit

3   Universities (or diaspora communities) to effectively translate knowledge in engineering, agriculture, technology, and other basic sciences into commercial innovation

The teams required for invention of R&D solutions are not always equipped to create companies that lead to job creation

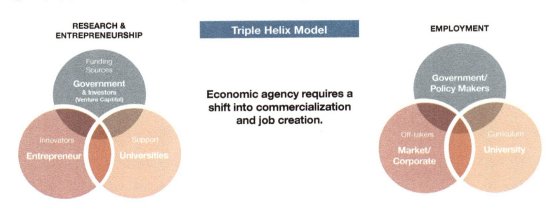

Used with permission from GreenHouse Capital

Today, Bunmi's focus is on transformation and job creation

I recently spent a week in Namibia with Bunmi Akinyemiju, where we shared many cups of coffee and met with university leaders from all over Africa to introduce a pilot designed to accelerate job creation. In conversation after conversation and site visit after site visit, I could feel the excitement as leaders stepped forward with open minds to consider an important challenge: How might universities, private sector and policy makers come together to build a robust employment ecosystem in Africa? What are new models that will tap into the continent's strengths and create jobs for the coming generation?

Stop to ask "why" before we plan to expand

As we're learning in this book, we all have different end games for innovation. Nicolas Cortázar needed a viable business model to replace Intergráficas' position as a leader in CD music production, a dying industry. As we'll learn shortly, Rappi, a Mexican company, was looking to expand by providing a suite of products and services that would close important gaps for their customers. They started with food delivery, evolved into payments, expanded into travel, and ultimately built out an omnichannel platform beyond their original geographical borders.

GreenHouse Capital's next step is optimized for job creation and Africa-based economic agency. As our capacity grows, our potential expands. But, before we race toward scale for scale's sake, we need to hit pause and ask: What is our motivation for expansion?

Before we race headlong into a growth strategy, we should first ask, "What are we optimizing for?" Once we're clear about the end game, it's easier to chart a path that's right for us.

TOOL: THE 4-BEAT STORY

We confront new and pressing challenges in this unfolding chapter of our journey.

 Purpose

Synthesize insights and aspirations into a crisp, action-oriented format. Allows a team to align on what's important, what the value is for various constituent groups, and how the initiative will be measured.

 How to use it + example

Work in teams or in a retreat setting to expand on the Four Quadrants from the Envision module. Frame the core concepts into four categories that make up a 4-Beat Story:

- **Beat 1:** The future need you're addressing and who you'll serve

- **Beat 2:** Description of the initiative(s)

- **Beat 3:** The impact/value you'll create

- **Beat 4:** Success metrics

Make sure to word it through the perspective of stakeholders and impact. Don't focus on what you will do (internal view: "how the watch is made"). Instead, focus on the value and impact you're creating.

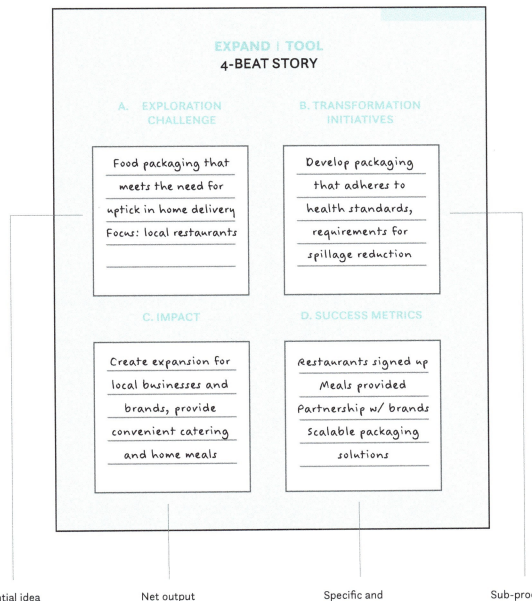

EXPAND | TOOL
4-BEAT STORY

A. EXPLORATION CHALLENGE

Food packaging that meets the need for uptick in home delivery Focus: local restaurants

B. TRANSFORMATION INITIATIVES

Develop packaging that adheres to health standards, requirements for spillage reduction

C. IMPACT

Create expansion for local businesses and brands, provide convenient catering and home meals

D. SUCCESS METRICS

Restaurants signed up
Meals provided
Partnership w/ brands
Scalable packaging solutions

Potential idea implemented and target audience

Net output of the idea explored

Specific and measurable milestones in the initiative

Sub-processes imperative to the execution of the tasks presented

Your turn: Instructions

Fill in the sections on the opposite page as follows:

A   **EXPLORATION CHALLENGE.** Turn your Four Quadrants (from Envision) into a narrative. In this first box, describe the challenge you will take on in a few bullet points. What will you solve? What future value will you bring to your customers? Tell the story of the unmet need you're hoping to address or the future value you'll bring to customers.

B   **TRANSFORMATION INITIATIVES.** Provide details on how you envision the new product or innovation. What will you do?

C   **IMPACT.** Describe the specific target and the value you'll bring to them. What is that value and who will benefit from it?

D   **SUCCESS METRICS.** How will you measure success? What will you point to as proof of your success? Be specific.

4-BEAT STORY

A. EXPLORATION CHALLENGE

B. TRANSFORMATION INITIATIVES

C. IMPACT

D. SUCCESS METRICS

NOTES

Key takeaway

This process translates the possibility of the Envision step into a format that can be tested and refined.

The 4-Beat Story provides a discipline to get everyone on the same page from the start.

What to do next

Now that your team is on the same page about your 4-Beat Story, let's talk about how we can stretch, immerse, and learn to expand it.

TOOL: EXPANDING THE 4-BEAT STORY

 Purpose

This tool is designed to help you crystallize your thinking; it provides immediate, high-level feedback for your initiative. Expanding the 4-Beat Story begins the process of broadening your perspectives to see new opportunities around your initiative. It also helps you to identify potential snags or areas of risk.

 How to use it + example

Shorten your 4-Beat Story from the last exercise into short segments and fill out the remaining fields of the tool. Then, set up one-on-one conversations, workshops, and feedback sessions to get input that expands your perspective.

Use a new worksheet for each conversation.

First, present the 4-Beat Story summary from the box at the top of the sheet.

Then, using the "No, but" box, invite people to share their concerns about your initiative. Ask them to consider logistical snags, budgetary challenges, and the potential for unknown issues to arise (cannibalizing your current products, for example).

After you've heard their feedback on snags and risks, show them the "Yes, and" field. Ask them to list ideas that would help you build momentum.

Finally, in the "Open Mind" field, set the tone for open brainstorming to build on the initiative. Use prompts like "How might we make this initiative even bolder?" or "What might we do for an even bigger impact?"

Succinct summary of the market, venture and measurable impact of potential product

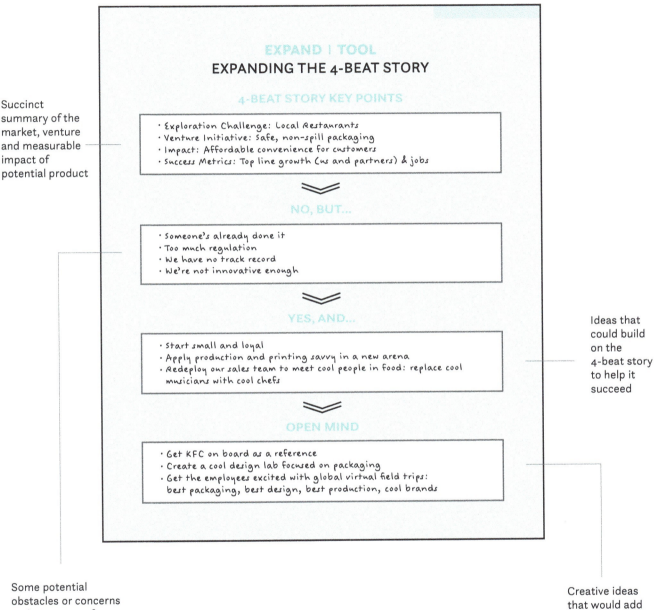

EXPANDING THE 4-BEAT STORY

4-BEAT STORY KEY POINTS

- Exploration Challenge: Local Restaurants
- Venture Initiative: Safe, non-spill packaging
- Impact: Affordable convenience for customers
- Success Metrics: Top line growth (us and partners) & jobs

NO, BUT...

- Someone's already done it
- Too much regulation
- We have no track record
- We're not innovative enough

YES, AND...

- Start small and loyal
- Apply production and printing savvy in a new arena
- Redeploy our sales team to meet cool people in food: replace cool musicians with cool chefs

OPEN MIND

- Get KFC on board as a reference
- Create a cool design lab focused on packaging
- Get the employees excited with global virtual field trips: best packaging, best design, best production, cool brands

Ideas that could build on the 4-beat story to help it succeed

Some potential obstacles or concerns in the process of expansion

Creative ideas that would add even greater impact

Your turn: Instructions

Fill in the sections on the opposite page as follows:

- **4-BEAT STORY KEY POINTS.** Distill your 4-Beat Story into a concise, compelling summary.

- **NO, BUT...** What potential negative feedback could arise from your team, organization, customers, or partners? What are their concerns and objections? Set a timer and brainstorm these challenges.

- **YES, AND...** How can you build on the original idea to enhance its potential? What opportunities can you identify using the "yes, and" technique from improvisational comedy? Set a timer and brainstorm these possibilities.

- **OPEN MIND.** How can you stretch your imagination to make the idea even bolder and more innovative? What creative ideas can you generate to enhance the original concept?

EXPANDING THE 4-BEAT STORY

4-BEAT STORY SUMMARY

-
-
-
-

≫

NO, BUT...

-
-
-
-

≫

YES, AND...

-
-
-
-

≫

OPEN MIND

-
-
-
-

NOTES

Key takeaway

Expanding the 4-Beat Story involves conversations, workshops, immersion sessions, and feedback from a wide range of people: customers, collaborators, technical experts, and colleagues. In every discussion, stretch the boundaries of what might be possible. The key is to listen and explore, not edit or judge.

What to do next

Continue to expand your 4-Beat Story using the Innovation Enablers tool, which we'll cover next.

TOOL: INNOVATION ENABLERS

As we continue to expand our 4-Beat Story, we'll explore three ways to transform early-stage ideas into scalable initiatives: 1) the integration of innovative technologies, 2) the introduction of novel business models, and 3) the application of best practices from other industries.

 ### Purpose

The goal of this exercise is to broaden your perspective through three important lenses: technology potential, business-model possibilities, and cross-industry inspiration. At the core of most strategic initiatives is a need to strengthen our internal capacity and capabilities; Innovation Enablers provide the structure. We help our teams focus on learning.

 ### How to use it + example

Expand your 4-Beat Story by researching and applying insights related to each category: technologies that could be applied, innovative business-model options, and best practices from other industries.

This process forces teams to invest time to dive deep enough into three critical areas to make informed decisions about where to start the next stage, Build.

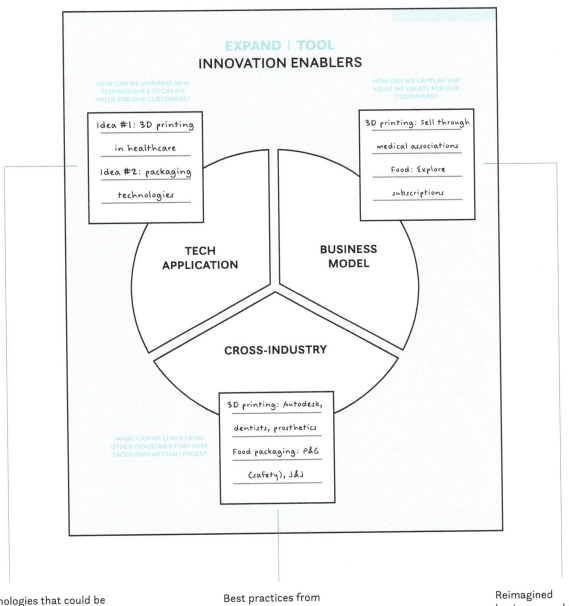

INNOVATION ENABLERS

HOW CAN WE LEVERAGE NEW
TECHNOLOGIES TO CREATE
VALUE FOR OUR CUSTOMERS?

HOW CAN WE CAPTURE THE
VALUE WE CREATE FOR OUR
CUSTOMERS?

Idea #1: 3D printing

in healthcare

Idea #2: packaging

technologies

3D printing: Sell through

medical associations

Food: Explore

subscriptions

TECH APPLICATION

BUSINESS MODEL

CROSS-INDUSTRY

WHAT CAN WE LEARN FROM
OTHER INDUSTRIES THAT HAVE
FACED SIMILAR CHALLENGES?

3D printing: Autodesk,

dentists, prosthetics

Food packaging: P&G

(safety), J&J

Technologies that could be
applied in the context of the
industry

Best practices from
other industries to
learn from

Reimagined
business-model
opportunites

Your turn: Instructions

Fill in the sections on the opposite page as follows:

- **TECH APPLICATION.** Assign a team to research new technologies such as AI, advanced manufacturing, and university-based inventions. List promising technologies you might apply to advance your initiative.

- **BUSINESS MODEL.** Consider novel business models, including new distribution structures, payment options, and collaboration. List promising models here.

- **CROSS-INDUSTRY.** Assign a team to research leaders in other industries whose innovations might be applied to your project. For example, is there a platform in mobile phones that might be applied to your banking innovation?

INNOVATION ENABLERS

HOW CAN WE LEVERAGE NEW
TECHNOLOGIES TO CREATE
VALUE FOR OUR CUSTOMERS?

HOW CAN WE CAPTURE THE
VALUE WE CREATE FOR OUR
CUSTOMERS?

**TECH
APPLICATION**

**BUSINESS
MODEL**

CROSS-INDUSTRY

WHAT CAN WE LEARN FROM
OTHER INDUSTRIES THAT HAVE
FACED SIMILAR CHALLENGES?

NOTES

Key takeaway

Significant expansion and scale opportunities come from learning about the successes of other companies and organizations. Traditional strategy focuses on our own industries, but the truth is that incumbent banks (for example) can learn a lot from companies that are not banks. The faster path to scaling new initiatives is to study these enablers, interview people from other companies, and master some of the skills (for example, running a virtual platform) that have led to success for others and apply them to your own organization.

What to do next

Continue to expand the 4-Beat Story using the Opportunity Aperture, which provides a deeper exploration using inspiration from specific companies in critical strategic areas.

TOOL: OPPORTUNITY APERTURE

 Purpose

To elevate our level of impact, our companies need to take best practices from companies outside of our industry. What can an insurance company learn from other insurance companies about online customer service compared to what they might learn from Amazon? This tool is designed to inspire you to think of areas where you need to excel and to research examples of companies who are leading the pack in those capabilities to raise the standard of your own game.

 How to use it + example

First, list six areas where you'd need to excel to implement or scale your initiative. Do you need to become great at supply chain relationships? Maybe you believe growth can come through global distribution. Is product development speed an emerging priority for your customers?

There are elements of our future strategies that have already been modeled by companies outside our four walls and often successfully achieved by companies outside of our industry.

The Opportunity Aperture equips us to focus on a small set of capabilities (in this example, six) that we know will drive our progress forward and then study organizations that have paved the way for us to apply those strategies to our own initiatives.

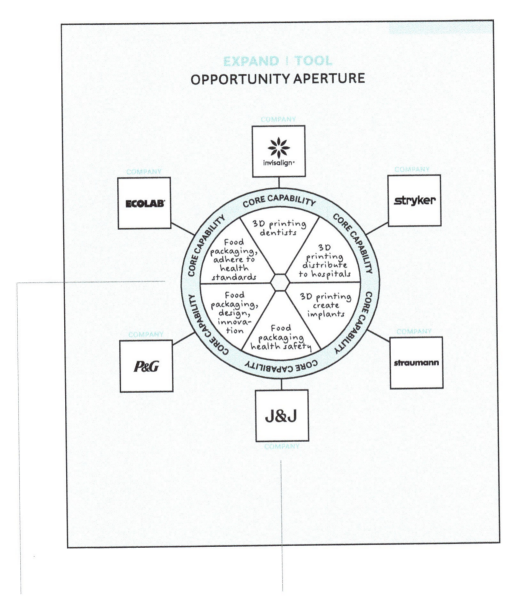

OPPORTUNITY APERTURE

Core capability
that can be applied

Example of a
company with
that core
capability

Your turn: Instructions

Fill in the sections on the opposite page
as follows:

- **CORE CAPABILITIES.** What are some core
  capabilities that could strengthen your
  initiative? Write these in the pie-shaped
  sections at the center of the page.

- **COMPANIES.** What are some companies
  from other industries that exemplify best
  practices regarding each core capability that
  could be replicable in your organization?

OPPORTUNITY APERTURE

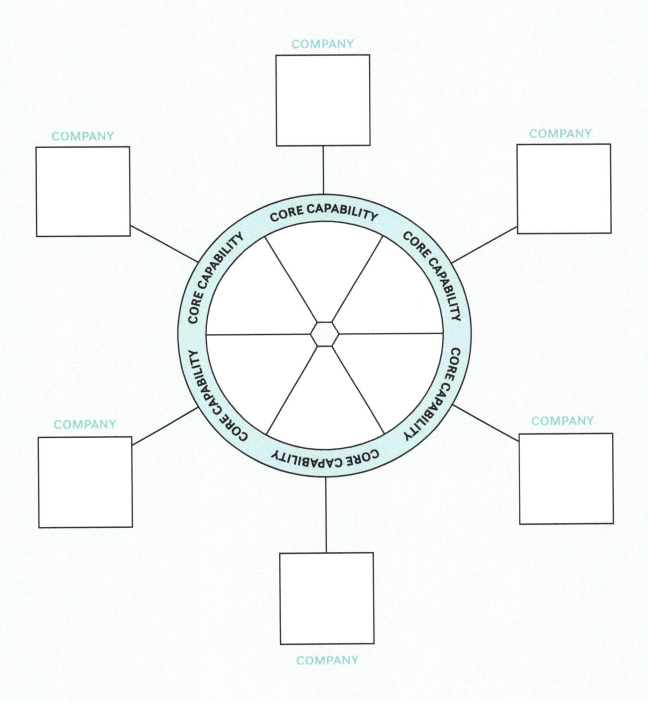

NOTES

Key takeaway

To achieve higher levels of impact and innovation, organizations should proactively seek inspiration and best practices from companies outside their own industry, identifying areas where they need to excel and studying organizations that have successfully pioneered those capabilities to elevate their own standards and drive progress.

What to do next

This exercise can be done in multiple cycles. It's designed as a guide for an individual, a team, or even an organization to start plotting insights about how other companies have achieved (at least in part) each of the components of their future strategy. You can begin to model a "Frankenstein" combination with the best practices from each component to inform your planning.

In the coming Build stage, you can model or simulate some of the ideas. For example, how might you build an ecosystem like the one Airbnb has built to add value to many players in your sphere of influence at once?

Apply the highest standards from each inspirational company to build your concept bigger.

TOOL: IDEABOARD

 Purpose

This tool is designed to integrate your expanded insights into a single framework.

 How to use it + example

Applying the ideas from the Expand section, express your expanded vision for your initiative prompted by the fields on the Ideaboard.

In this exercise, you'll start by considering the emerging customer needs, trends, and technologies you'll be building on. You'll then describe the idea itself along with the initial business model you'll test and make note of cross-industry companies you'll consider in your own execution. Finally, you'll articulate any burning questions that need to be answered and jot notes that may be helpful to remember later.

Noted shift in the market and how product would address the new landscape

Summary of what you'll do and for whom

EXPAND | TOOL
IDEABOARD

EMERGING SHIFTS: CUSTOMERS, MARKET

Food won't go off trend

Delivery apps offer a new channel for restaurants, issues with packaging

IDEA

We will create the leading food packaging and delivery support company in LATAM

TRENDS YOU'LL BUILD ON

Delivery network, At-home eating, Catering in-office

BUSINESS MODEL ELEMENTS

Begin with restaurants as a back-end infrastructure partner

TECHNOLOGIES YOU'LL EXPLORE

Payment apps, Logistics platforms, Safety reporting and testing

CROSS-MODEL ELEMENTS

Ecolab safety standards, P&G packaging innovation, J&J distribution model

BURNING QUESTIONS

· How might we outpace the innovation already provided in the market?

· What will it take to get long-term contracts from brands like KFC?

· Where are the gaps in food packaging that provide sustainable growth potential?

NOTES

· Address the employee issue: will food be appealing to the sales team as an industry?

· Learn about the food safety requirements

· Explore packaging as innovatively as possible

· Take field trips

· Talk with KFC

Aspects of the new trend that could support your growth

Key operational elements

Potential tech that could mesh with trends

Key questions to be addressed before launch

Potential snags, creative ideas to explore, critical reminders

What you'll borrow from other industries

Fill in the sections on the opposite page
as follows:

- **EMERGING SHIFTS.** List the forces that are
  driving the new project.

- **TRENDS YOU'LL BUILD ON.** Highlight the
  trends that will provide momentum.

- **TECHNOLOGIES TO EXPLORE.** Summarize
  the technologies you'll be applying.

- **IDEA.** Summarize the new project.

- **BUSINESS MODEL ELEMENTS.** Describe the
  business model you'll test.

- **CROSS-MODEL ELEMENTS.** List the cross-industry best practices: companies that are
  already excelling at one or more aspects of
  what you're going to do.

- **BURNING QUESTIONS.** Write down the questions you'll need to address in the upcoming
  Build stage.

- **NOTES.** List additional concerns, comments,
  and reminders not covered by the other boxes.

EXPAND | TOOL
IDEABOARD

EMERGING SHIFTS: CUSTOMERS, MARKET

-
-
-

IDEA

-
-
-

TRENDS YOU'LL BUILD ON

-
-

BUSINESS MODEL ELEMENTS

-
-

TECHNOLOGIES TO EXPLORE

-

CROSS-MODEL ELEMENTS

-

BURNING QUESTIONS

-
-
-

NOTES

-
-
-

NOTES

Key takeaway

The Ideaboard starts with facts and hypotheses related to the opportunity space: customer, market, and societal forces that point to an environment that's conducive to a new initiative. Then, the team articulates the trends they've identified that support change. To enrich these, it helps to collect all the information in one place so that new team members have a reference point for the initial assumptions.

The team should revisit and update this Ideaboard throughout the upcoming Build module.

What to do next

Share the concepts in a group to build them bigger and bolder and gain different people's insights and criticisms.

SPOTLIGHT STORY: RAPPI
The Secret to Billion-dollar Growth

Rappi's formula rests on converting hidden customer desires into essential commerce

I first heard about Rappi in a meeting with Mario Hernandez from OpenFinance, Mexico. The discussion was about how large banks might leapfrog into open banking. Mario told me about a small company called Rappi that had a payments plugin that might become an ingredient in the overall customer solution. Many scaleup companies offered niche solutions to banks at the time, so I didn't make much of Mario's tip about Rappi but filed them away in my mind as a company to watch.

A few months later, I heard about Rappi again in a different context: this time from Pete Comeau from Phocuswright, a travel industry organization. I told Pete I was interested in how travel companies could earn customer trust with enough credibility to convert them from small-ticket purchases to larger-ticket ones and increase customer loyalty. How could travel companies avoid "fickle customer syndrome?"

I was surprised when Pete suggested I talk to Guido Becher, head of travel for Rappi. Could the same company innovating in the banking sector be a leader in a different industry? I'll never forget my first video call with Guido, where he shared the common threads connecting the company's successes in what seemed like unrelated disciplines. It's a story of expanding by establishing deep customer trust and applying unrivaled insights to emerging and unmet customer needs.

Have you ever wished you could wave a wand to discover unmet customer needs? That's the secret sauce Rappi used to expand through a strategy built around customer trust.

It's all too common to start building immediately after we finish whiteboarding an idea. But that's nearly a guarantee that we'll be besieged by blind spots and waste time on prototypes that don't satisfy underlying customer needs. Before we build, we need to apply tools to ensure we're not simply building products that will become me-toos.

The Expand tools provide a structured process to open our minds to insights from other industries, imagine novel applications of technologies and business models, and apply emerging trends to our early-stage ideas.

Rappi applied this Expand mindset to establish a powerful growth model. Over the course of more than five years, they grew from a humble sandwich delivery service into a company with a game-changing superpower: the ability to uncover hidden customer needs and translate them into high-growth, high-impact lines of business.

Secrets to scaling a company: Rappi nails emerging available markets and expands from food to travel and beyond

It's 2015. On the streets of Bogotá, a small team of hawkers is giving away donuts for free. All you have to do is download an app—right there, on the spot—and get a donut. The company is brand new, and the founders of Rappi have a big idea: Let's make it easy for people to get lunch delivered by bicycle all over Bogotá.

The idea of mobile app food delivery was hardly new. Companies like Grubhub have been around since 2004; Meituan was established in China in 2010, and by 2014 it already had 5,000 employees; Deliveroo, a UK-based company, came on the scene in 2013 and was on a dramatic growth trajectory. But no one other than Rappi was handing out donuts for free in Bogotá at the time.

Ever since those enthusiastic hawker days, Rappi has experienced a lot of growth and success. They've also delivered lots of lunches. There have been 100 million downloads (that's a lot of donuts). Rappi has 40,000 connected businesses on its platform. They have successfully branched out into arenas and industries that would be impossible to anticipate if you applied a traditional "stick-to-your-lane" strategy.

Luckily, Rappi ignored conventional views of how to scale and instead focused on a superpower that drove expansion—insight into what I call Emerging Available Markets (EAMs). Earning the trust of their customers to share their emerging unmet needs fueled Rappi's transformation from its original market position as a basic food delivery service to its current state as a multi-geography platform.

Here's how it worked.

Rappi's favor gets to the heart of the business

Mid-afternoon on a Tuesday in Bogotá, Guido Becher's son called him with a plea: "Dad, I left my football cleats at home and I've got to have them for after-school practice!"

Guido realized that to get the cleats from his house to his son's school required a motorbike that could weave through dense urban traffic.

"The superpower for growth in today's market comes from a combination of deep customer trust and a nimble organization that can provide for customers' unmet needs. That's how we have expanded from sandwich delivery into an omnichannel platform that supplies travel, entertainment and financial services. One customer insight at a time."

GUIDO BECHER
Global Head of Travel, Rappi

And Guido didn't have one. But he remembered a service called Rappi Favor that might make the magic happen. They advertised as "Need a Favor? We'll walk your dog or get some keys you left at work. Leave it to us."

So, Guido decided to broadcast the errand he needed to make his son's day to Rappi Favor.

Success. The cleats arrived on time and Guido's son had a great football practice.

More importantly, that moment sparked a bold insight. Guido realized Rappi's true power was much bigger than a quick delivery of sports shoes: once a company earns customer trust and nails the favor, it'll likely be trusted for other transactions. All the favors people were searching for represented potential lines of expansion. Which groupings of unmet needs might indicate a new branch for Rappi?

From a sushi lunch to a ticket to Tokyo

As founder and director of Netactica (the leading travel technology company in the Latin American region) since 2003, Guido was well-versed in the challenges of customer acquisition and the uphill battle required to earn the trust that would translate to longer-term loyalty.

Meanwhile, Rappi was tapping into deep motivations and real services that might warrant broader support. After all, if Rappi could aggregate all of the people whose children needed something they forgot, what else might those people need? Pharmacy deliveries in the middle of the night? Last-minute birthday gifts? Might it be possible to test a path that would start with lunch and end up with an airplane ticket?

Using the technology of Netactica as a starting point, Rappi was able to quickly experiment with new directions that might lead to expanding the market they serve and the lifetime value of their clients in a new vertical. After months of exploration, they landed on a surprising result: many people who ordered ceviche had hidden desires to travel to Peru. Not only that, but that hidden desire translated into airplane tickets that Rappi successfully provided to satisfy that customer need. Sushi orders translated to trips to Tokyo.

By uncovering an unmet need and providing a trusted way to scratch the travel itch, a new division was born: Rappi Travel. Today, Guido Becher is their Global Head of Travel.

Rappi continued to grow by applying the same formula, identifying emerging markets and partnering with innovative leaders whose capabilities would jumpstart a new line of business. Today, Rappi is a $5.25 billion enterprise that has successfully branched into games and live events and expanded their fintech and logistics offerings.

When interpreted correctly, data on existing customers uncovers opportunities for growth—areas that are ripe for cross-sector business expansion and new business models.

AT A GLANCE: RAPPI

TOPIC	Rappi began as a sandwich delivery service and evolved into an omnichannel platform with expertise in financial transactions, logistics, travel, and other verticals.
FROM STUCK TO SCALE STEP	Expand
WHERE PEOPLE GOT STUCK	Limiting their thinking about growth as a linear path within the original industry, sandwich delivery.
HOW THE *FROM STUCK TO SCALE* APPROACH WORKS BETTER THAN THE TRADITIONAL STRATEGY	Tools for expansion like SWOT begin with our own companies and focus on today's core competencies. *From Stuck to Scale* tools begin with emerging customer needs, market conditions, and important trends that will set the stage for future growth.
BREAKTHROUGH MOMENT	Recognizing that customers ordering sushi had unmet needs for flights to Tokyo.
IMPACT	By uncovering unmet customer needs, they landed on Emerging Available Markets and migrated from sandwich delivery to travel (and are now an omni-channel platform).
KEY INSIGHT	A company that earns trust in one arena (food delivery) could be given permission to expand their customer footprint into another arena (travel, fintech).
HOW YOU CAN APPLY THIS	Put the brakes on the temptation to rush into building prototypes right after brain-storming sessions. Instead, discipline your teams to uncover unmet needs and to search for partners, technologies or business models that might address those unmet needs.
FINAL TIP	Use tools like Opportunity Aperture to strengthen your offerings before you start building and testing.

Stretch your thinking beyond your industry like Rappi did as they branched out strategically from their origins as a sandwich delivery service. Discover the unmet and emerging customer needs—otherwise called Emerging Available Markets—as clues to where the market might be heading. Establish strong hypotheses to test in the next stage: Build.

CHAPTER SUMMARY

>> Key insights

The second stage of the *From Stuck to Scale* process, Expand, focuses on broadening perspectives through technology, business-model exploration, and cross-industry inspiration to unlock untapped growth opportunities.

>> Key Stuck Points

STUCK POINTS: FRICTION, RESISTANCE, OBSTACLES, CHALLENGES	TOOL TO USE	HOW IT WORKS
It's hard to tell a crisp, unified story about the challenge or transformation you want to take on.	The 4-Beat Story	Synthesizes many possible new directions into one clear description.
You need to stretch the possibilities beyond the team's initial framing.	Expanding the 4-Beat Story	A structured way to capture input that addresses blind spots and broadens the scope of your initial concept.
You struggle to apply new tech, novel go-to-market strategies, or external best practices.	Innovation Enablers	Forces you to apply three specific lenses: technology, business models, and cross-industry.
You're in a fixed mindset with your own company at the moment. You're stuck in SWOT thinking.	Opportunity Aperture	Look at non-industry peers to advance your innovation progress. Example: a healthcare company learns from Geek Squad's at-home tech support when shifting from hospital- to home-based care. Identify: 1) the shift required, 2) the future capabilities needed, 3) companies to benchmark against.
You need a simple summary to set the stage for experimentation in the upcoming Build phase. You struggle to define the questions that will drive go/no-go decisions.	Ideaboard	The first framework to describe the assumptions you'll test in the next stage. Building it takes a systematic process: summarize key assumptions, describe the idea, then craft burning questions you'll focus on in the upcoming test-and-learn experiments in step 3: Build.

>> Key actions

Use the 4-Beat Story worksheet to craft a compelling narrative that guides the innovation journey and aligns stakeholders on the initiative's value and impact.

>> Key question

The key question to address in this chapter is:

"How can we stretch our boundaries, immerse ourselves in technology-driven growth, and adopt innovative business models to maximize our potential for transformation and impact?"

>> Commitment

Commit to continually expanding the 4-Beat Story by exploring and applying insights related to technology potential, innovative business models, and cross-industry best practices, ensuring a comprehensive understanding and readiness for the upcoming Build stage.

We can't afford
to be the fastest
snail in a snail race.
Cross-industry
insights fix that.

STEP 3

BUILD
GROUNDING
IN REALITY

GOAL: Make it real: learn,
shift gears, modify, and debug

WHERE MIGHT YOU BE STUCK?

In this chapter, we'll address some of the following Stuck Points—friction, resistance, obstacles, and challenges—that may sound something like this:

- "We're stuck in blue-sky thinking and can't get real."

- "We're unsure how to test assumptions."

- "We don't know how to assess progress with key experiments."

- "Our early experiments didn't work out. How do we redirect our testing?"

- "Our team can't push beyond our blind spots."

Unsure where your situation fits in?

Visit www.andreakates.com/diagnostic and take the *From Stuck to Scale* Diagnostic to take stock.

Nail it before
you scale it.

T WAS TRICKY for Intergráficas to progress from the Expand stage to the Build stage. The teams got stuck in multiple ways. First, they had an unconscious preference for staying in the music industry. After all, that's what attracted them to their jobs to begin with. The fun of festivals, the sexiness of working with musicians, the allure of the perks and parties all pointed toward building prototypes that would keep both feet firmly in music.

Despite that strong pull, Nicolas forced the team to give other directions a chance. Might there be a strength they could double down on that would have more staying power than music? Could they redesign their manufacturing facility to produce something else? Would a new technology like 3D printing have legs?

Over the course of six months, teams learned, talked with hundreds of people, and visited customers and partners. To create low-cost prototypes in 3D printing, they immersed themselves in additive manufacturing and dentistry. Nicolas came to California to do site visits to digital health firms. The teams took their assignment seriously, filling in experiment journals and reflecting on what they were learning.

Every few weeks, we compared results. We included investors and outside experts in the progress review sessions. The teams ruled out the 3D manufacturing initiative because it was too complicated. Disappointingly to lots of people, most of the music-related projects were axed; the market size simply wasn't big enough.

After a few months, the teams reviewed the Experiment Tracker and applied the Uncover Opportunities framework that you're about to learn about to land on an emerging hot possibility that was lying in plain view, but that required a fresh mindset to define: Intergráficas might be in a position to apply one of their hidden gems—a fully optimized, six sigma-certified printing facility—to print something other than CD covers.

The Build stage culminated with a surprising result: Intergráficas would pursue printing food packaging as their path to get unstuck. They had one small relationship with KFC that might serve as a pilot to test their hypothesis.

The next few months were spent creating samples, researching health code requirements, and meeting dozens of potential customers who had nothing to do with music. They produced small print runs of bags and boxes.

Nicolas was aware that no solution would work if employees didn't embrace it and find a way to contribute. To keep the excitement alive with Intergráficas team members who loved music, they set up challenges to create innovative designs for sustainable packaging. Nicolas deployed the sales team to meet with restaurant owners and food-stand entrepreneurs to understand the challenges of temperature controls. Collectively, Intergráficas forged exciting relationships with a whole new community to conduct pilots.

They were poised to move from Build toward step 4: Engage.

THERE'S A moment in the pursuit of a new direction, the introduction of a new product, or advocacy for transformation, when we need to take concrete first steps. We need to move from the theoretical to the real. Luckily, we can rely on some skills from disciplines like design thinking to help us tap into customer needs and build prototypes. We can apply lean-startup knowledge to help us get started on a big idea with a small first step and start to experiment, test, and learn. Those disciplines are valuable as a point of departure.

The problem comes in the next stage, when things aren't working as planned. That's where the Build tools are critical. Build gives people specific guidance on where to pivot, and how to address blind spots and unintentional biases that keep us stuck. Build also confronts the truth about how to scale innovation—there can be a big leap from a small-scale experiment that works to a truly scalable line of business, company, platform, or purpose-driven initiative.

The ideal way to work with the Build tools is through a combination of individual work and team discussion. You'll progress your initial ideas from early-stage descriptions through to a clearer view of where you believe you and your team or organization could increase your impact.

The initiatives you work through can be internal or external. There might be an internal transformation initiative that you're considering, or a new customer-facing concept, line of business, or innovative business model.

To truly go *From Stuck to Scale*, we need to build in a new way that surrounds our ideas with the scaffolding and support that will drive us past stuck and lead to scale. The secret is to build within a context of diverse expertise, with a future focus, and to bring skills that open our minds to what it takes to bring an early-stage idea to scale.

In any application of the Build frameworks, the process of learning by doing begins here.

Your practical toolkit

The Build step shows you how to make your initiative real, learn from errors, shift gears, modify your goals, and debug any potential problems. In this chapter, we have five canvases and a bonus checklist.

Ideaboard (Part 2)

Completes your Ideaboard by translating your hunches into experiments. Defines tests that can accelerate learning.

Experiment Tracker

Evaluates your experiments from multiple perspectives. Surrounds you with mentors, guides, and experts. What are the facts that matter? How can you validate assumptions?

Untapped Opportunities

Guides qualitative interviews and discerns untapped opportunities. Where are there unspoken, unmet, emerging needs that are coming into focus?

Scale Optimizer Checklist

Moves you from early-stage pilots to a fully scaled size and scope.

Bias and Blind Spot Tracker

Identifies blind spots and biases that directly affect experiment evaluation. Where are we missing the truth?

BONUS: Experiment Pressure Tester Checklist

We also included a bonus sheet to help you pressure test your experiments.

Building for the future starts with learning.

SPOTLIGHT STORY: HILTI
Corporate Portfolios

*How to build a strong portfolio
and acquisitions that thrive*

It was such a beautiful day in Barcelona that I almost felt guilty herding people from the sunny balcony of a historic building into a conference room for a strategy session. Fortunately, the energy in the room stayed high as we started discussing corporate innovation. The group hailed from around the world, conversation was multilingual, and the topics we discussed ranged from successes to stumbling blocks. One of the most compelling participants was Antonia Elisa Soler Blasco, a Barcelona native who worked for Hilti, a family-owned, Liechtenstein-based company focused on construction.

What impressed me about Antonia was that her questions aimed directly at how to build corporate portfolios with the right mix of initiatives, partnerships, ventures, technologies, products, services, and innovation. My workshop that day focused on how to overcome "stuck," and Antonia got to the heart of the challenges and opportunity costs faced by a large organization when placing their innovation bets.

After that meeting, Antonia and I stayed in touch. It turned out that she worked in San Francisco, where I live. I knew about Hilti's track record from reading a case study about their tools fleet management success, which underscored the company's nimbleness in applying novel business models. I was curious about how Hilti thought about the Build stage in today's market environment, and met with Antonia to understand how to build a strong software portfolio. What she shared was fascinating.

Differentiation beyond hardware

The Hilti Group supplies the worldwide construction industry with technologically leading products, systems, software, and services. With about 34,000 team members in over 120 countries, the company stands for direct customer relationships, quality, and innovation.

Construction is one of the largest industries globally. It plays a central role in the world economy, creating jobs for millions of people, providing housing to almost everyone on the planet, and building commercial, industrial, and civil infrastructures that enable economic growth. The industry, however, faces significant challenges that require it to transform.

Because of the magnitude of the effort required to both apply new technologies and stay ahead of volatile market forces, customers are looking for true partners to sit side-by-side with them, not simply firms who respond to bids. With its focus on innovation, Hilti is ideally positioned to be just such a partner and help its customers do things better. That is why Hilti has defined "Making Construction Better" as its purpose, and aims to be its customers' best partner for productivity, safety, and sustainability.

Originally, Hilti's efforts were targeted to help construction workers perform their tasks faster, easier, and safer—and hence become more productive through their jobsite applications. Today, this commitment to continuous innovation is evident in Hilti's diverse range of cutting-edge tools, technologies, services, and software that redefine industry standards and drive efficiency.

The path from Hilti's origins to their current focus on tools, hardware, software, and other innovations evolved organically, driven in large part by a strong desire to serve customers. Hilti had traditionally been a hardware company with strong differentiation and a direct sales force. But they realized that they had to take that differentiation beyond the product if they wanted to continue offering strong value and stay relevant for their customers. Hilti's twenty-year success with fleet management (aka Fleet) is a prime example of a solution that drives jobsite productivity in a holistic way. Fleet customers pay a monthly fee to access the tools they need. In exchange, they benefit from repair services, loaner tools, and the availability of additional tools required for peak project times. Hilti was transitioning from simply a product supplier who offered some related services to a provider of hardware as a service, making them a true productivity partner to their customers.

The next step was to offer software as a service with ON!Track, a robust asset management system designed to help businesses track and manage their tools and equipment efficiently. Software as a service was a new domain for Hilti, but was still within their area of expertise: managing tools and equipment. Together, Fleet and ON!Track form a unique offering that helps construction companies manage their tool parks professionally, allowing them to focus on their core business.

The success of Fleet and ON!Track showed that Hilti could build a software business and that services and software drive engagement, allowing Hilti to have a bigger impact on their customers' businesses. They were also key building blocks to future innovation that have positioned Hilti to be at the forefront of digitalization in the construction industry.

Hilti builds a software business

Taking a leading role in driving productivity through digitalization requires a strong software play. Within their software development strategy, project management was identified as an important capability that Hilti needed to possess. To ramp up quickly and benefit from a mature product, Hilti acquired Fieldwire, a jobsite management software that connects the field to the office, enabling efficient and real-time information sharing from the foremen to the project managers and everyone in between. Fieldwire and Hilti were targeting similar customers, and both shared the goal of improving jobsite productivity.

The working relationship that developed between the two companies helped shine light on Hilti's new software strategy and identify Fieldwire as the most promising candidate to build Hilti's project management software. Equally, Fieldwire could also see that Hilti was the right company to help them scale their business and accelerate growth through its direct sales force and access to customers. The next step for the Hilti and Fieldwire teams was to successfully integrate their businesses. Hilti's employees, from the sales force to the operations teams, had to see Fieldwire's team as an integral part of the company fabric, not merely an add-on technology.

According to Michael Neidow, Business Unit Head, Construction Software, nothing can be left to chance in such an integration. Between 2017 and 2021, when Hilti acquired Fieldwire for $300 million, a large part of the effort has been spent on building trust and augmenting the cultural fit. The same has been true since the acquisition, but to an even greater extent.

Hilti and Fieldwire work on a successful integration

Almost three years later, the results have been outstanding. The Hilti and Fieldwire teams have been working side-by-side since the acquisition, achieving their milestones while maintaining exceptionally high employee retention. Today, the company is three times the size it was in terms of revenue, number of employees, and number of customers. What has been the key to this success? The answer is clear: strategy, culture, and execution.

Strategy

- **Strong business rationale.** The strategic logic to develop a software business within Hilti was clear. Additionally, Fieldwire was a category leader with a proven market fit that would help anchor this new software strategy. At the same time, Fieldwire was planning to expand beyond the U.S. into Europe and reach its next level of scale and impact, and would benefit from Hilti's strong brand and worldwide footprint.

- **Complementary capabilities.** What Hilti had to offer—distribution, resources, brand, and European footprint—was exactly what Fieldwire needed. What Fieldwire had to offer—startup culture, software solution, digital distribution, and an agile development methodology—was just what Hilti was looking for. On top of that, Fieldwire's leadership was

> "The difference between deals that look good on paper but die an early death versus deals that thrive in the long run depends 100% on relationships and goals alignment. Building successful partnerships requires a very intentional and focused process aimed at implementing the strategic value drivers and bringing the companies together culturally".
>
> **MICHAEL NEIDOW**, Business Unit Head, Construction Software

excited about Hilti's plans to develop a software business and being part of building Hilti's future software offering.

- **Initiative led from the top.** Hilti's senior management was committed to building a software business. The strategy had been fully aligned with all key internal stakeholders, and everyone wanted it to succeed.

Culture

- **Pre-acquisition relationship.** An initial investment in Fieldwire allowed Hilti and Fieldwire to build trust over a four-year period. As a result, Hilti had already seen how Fieldwire operated and understood their capabilities.

- **Shared values and mission.** Both companies have a long-term approach, care about customers' experience and brand, and strive to build great products. They also share compatible cultures and act with honesty and openness.

- **Common goals.** Hilti understood that Fieldwire knew more about software and sought to learn from them. Equally, the Fieldwire founding team saw the value that Hilti could provide and stayed onboard for three years post-acquisition, which sent a positive message of continuity to their team.

Execution

- **Clear expectations.** During the acquisition process, expectations were clearly defined about how the companies would work together throughout the integration. Fieldwire continued to operate with full autonomy, and the integration was kept to just those that were mission critical.

- **Kept promises.** Promises kept included funding, results, support, and more. Fieldwire leadership kept running the business and Hilti's senior executives were there to help remove roadblocks. Fieldwire requested a mandate to operate differently, and Hilti understood that it was needed to successfully build a software business and get the best from the newly acquired company. Throughout the effort, they articulated three types of rules: 1) rules that were to be followed, 2) rules that were to be broken, and 3) rules that were yet to be rewritten.

To avoid getting stuck in a game of chance when building corporate innovation portfolios, make sure your team brings both corporate heft as well as scaleup nimbleness. And do not take culture for granted in making the partnership gel.

- **Centralized steering.** Both product development and go-to-market activity were jointly steered. This was unique at Hilti, as the company operates as a matrix organization with business units leading product development and market organizations leading go-to-market activities.

Hilti knows their strengths and recognizes the opportunities from partnering with others. But the component of Hilti's DNA that makes all the difference in building a portfolio with trusted scaleups comes from a deep appreciation for true collaboration. That DNA paved the way for Hilti to enhance its innovation portfolio with Fieldwire, which Michael Neidow describes as an example of how to rise above one of the key elements challenging the success of acquisitions: strategic focus on culture.

AT A GLANCE: HILTI

TOPIC	Hilti cultivates a high-performance acquisition through deep win-win commitment.
FROM STUCK TO SCALE STEP	Build
WHERE PEOPLE GOT STUCK	Bridging two cultures and continuing to evolve: the Hilti Group originally focused on delivering hardware for the construction industry, and is now committing to also provide software solutions to construction professionals.
HOW THE *FROM STUCK TO SCALE* APPROACH WORKS BETTER THAN TRADITIONAL STRATEGY	Too often, traditional acquisitions suffer from the belief that deals on paper are the same as deals with people. Blind-spot tracking uncovers the areas that matter to the people on both sides of the deal.
BREAKTHROUGH MOMENT	The "DNA Match." From the time of investment to the time of acquisition, Hilti's executive team was fully committed to making this strategic partnership a joint success by building on shared values and bringing the companies together culturally.
IMPACT	The team has achieved all sales growth targets, and in three years has tripled the size of the business. Fieldwire has heavily expanded in Europe. In less than three years they will have gone from having a physical presence in two countries to being present in twenty countries. The founders and executive team have been on board for three years, coached their successors, and prepared for a smooth transition.
KEY INSIGHT	No matter how good a deal looks on paper, it will never work unless both parties get value from the partnership that could never have been achieved without the other party. In the case of Hilti and Fieldwire, that value began when they experienced true collaborative spirit.
HOW YOU CAN APPLY THIS	Corporate leaders and innovative scaleups need to look beyond the spreadsheets and invest time in the DNA match: relationships, trust, mutual benefit, and long-term value.
FINAL TIP	Make sure your portfolio strategy addresses culture match and brings outsized value to each partner.

"The reality is that most acquisitions don't go well. Hilti was very clear about their objectives when they acquired Fieldwire. That clarity empowered us to challenge the status quo when needed by simply asking: Is this good for the business? Is this helping us achieve our goal?"

YVES FRINAULT AND JAVED SINGHA, Fieldwire Founders

TOOL: IDEABOARD (PART 2)

 ## Purpose

During the Envision step, you filled in Part One of an Ideaboard with an overview of your initiative, transformation project, commercialization concept, or impact project. Now you'll break it down into experiments that will either validate your hunches or send you in a new direction. It's critical to evaluate your initiative from the perspective of the people who will benefit, who will pay for it, and who need or want it. Be sure to think about the concept from *their* perspective.

 ## How to use it + example

Complete this with your team or group through a series of strategic planning sessions. Fill in the top four boxes first. Then, in the remaining boxes, you'll write high-level descriptions of the experiments you'll run and add any "ahas," actions, or accelerants.

Too many projects begin from the perspective of what we want to make or how we can make incremental improvements to products or services we already have. By contrast, the Ideaboard forces teams to put the customer's unmet needs upfront and in the equation. The solutions need to bring value that someone will pay for, engage with, and continue to support over time.

Customer-seen value

Simple description of solution

BUILD | TOOL
IDEABOARD - YOUR INITATIVE
JOB TO BE DONE

Make food packaging delivery perfection: spillage, temperature, safety

⌄⌄

SOLUTION

Top-quality, innovative containers and backend infrastructure

⌄⌄

PAINS & GAINS

Today's packaging is retrofitted and not optimized for massive delivery needs

⌄⌄

FEATURES & ATTRIBUTES

· Safe, snazzy, spillage-free, temperature-controlled, board of health-approved
· Added plus: end customers crave it (Gamified? Attractive? Collectable?)

⌄⌄

VALIDATIONS & EXPERIMENTS

· Local rollout with friendlies in Bogotá
· Initial runs with small-scale prototypes for feedback
· Trial with KFC

⌄⌄

AHAS, ACTIONS, ACCELERANTS

· Create a "Frankenstein" combination of best practices with cross-industry inspiration

Where customers feel the most need for growth

Distinctiveness about product

Potential catalysts for growth

Potential testing opportunities

Your turn: Instructions

Complete the worksheet as follows:

- **JOB TO BE DONE.** What value is there for the customer? What is the "job to be done" that your solution will achieve?

- **SOLUTION.** What is your actual solution?

- **PAINS & GAINS.** Which pains does your customer currently experience that your initiative will tackle? How will they measure the gains from your new solution?

- **FEATURES & ATTRIBUTES.** What exactly will your product features be? What are the attributes of your service?

- **VALIDATIONS & EXPERIMENTS.** What will your experiments look like to test and learn? Fill in up to three versions.

- **AHAS, ACTIONS, ACCELERANTS.** As you begin to make progress with your experiments, update this box to summarize your insights.

BUILD | TOOL
IDEABOARD – YOUR INITATIVE

JOB TO BE DONE

-
-

⌄⌄

SOLUTION

-
-

⌄⌄

PAINS & GAINS

-
-

⌄⌄

FEATURES & ATTRIBUTES

-
-

⌄⌄

VALIDATIONS & EXPERIMENTS

-
-

⌄⌄

AHAS, ACTIONS, ACCELERANTS

-
-

NOTES

Key takeaway

There are multiple opportunities for any company to succeed. With an ecosystem play, it will be important to validate the priorities of each party independently and then convene the team regularly to build continued growth opportunities for everyone.

What to do next

Develop the high-level validation experiments into a set of test-and-learn sprints. Track progress on the Experiment Tracker.

TOOL: EXPERIMENT TRACKER

 ## Purpose

Summarize insights from your test-and-learn experiments. Use one form for each experiment. The form is designed to document the experimentation process and to impose discipline on the teams to assess critical milestones, discuss which assumptions have been validated, and evaluate implications. In addition to this tracker, every team should keep lab journals with more detailed notes on the experiments.

 ## How to use it + example

After a critical stage of an experiment, gather the team for a review. Use the following categories to guide the process:

- "What we thought," "What we did," and "What we learned," provide a general learning summary

- "Significant verbatims" force the team to document exact quotes from qualitative tests

- "Value drivers" direct attention to the economic insights

- "Future spark" documents themes that point to the potential for a new concept based on imagined future value

- "Book of facts" is a place to record strategic data that emerges

It's critical to combine data, observations, facts, verbatims, and concrete results into insights about what to do next. The value is for a team to discuss and align what was learned and synthesize it into a short list in the "What to Do Next" box.

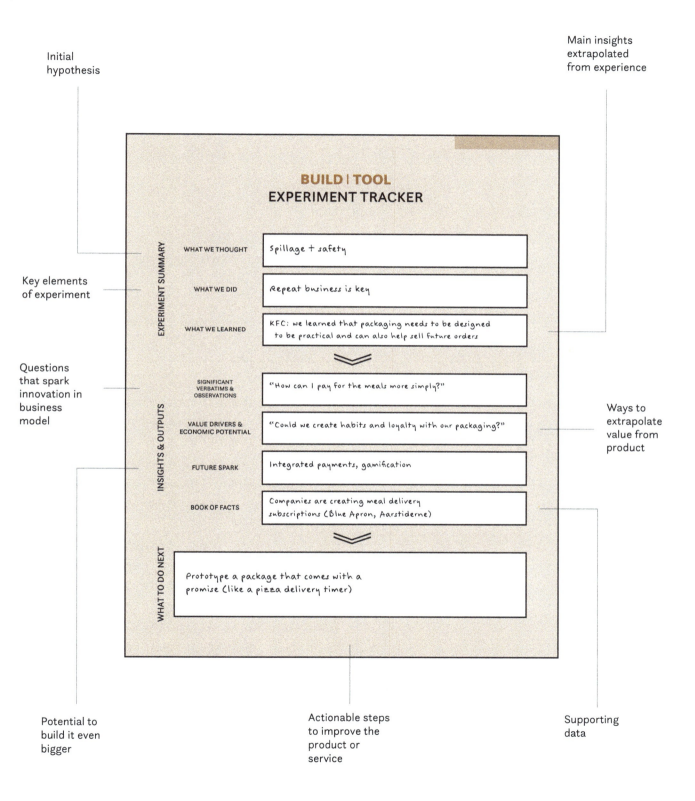

Initial hypothesis

Main insights extrapolated from experience

Key elements of experiment

Questions that spark innovation in business model

Ways to extrapolate value from product

BUILD | TOOL
EXPERIMENT TRACKER

EXPERIMENT SUMMARY

WHAT WE THOUGHT
Spillage + safety

WHAT WE DID
Repeat business is key

WHAT WE LEARNED
KFC: we learned that packaging needs to be designed to be practical and can also help sell future orders

INSIGHTS & OUTPUTS

SIGNIFICANT VERBATIMS & OBSERVATIONS
"How can I pay for the meals more simply?"

VALUE DRIVERS & ECONOMIC POTENTIAL
"Could we create habits and loyalty with our packaging?"

FUTURE SPARK
Integrated payments, gamification

BOOK OF FACTS
Companies are creating meal delivery subscriptions (Blue Apron, Aarstiderne)

WHAT TO DO NEXT

Prototype a package that comes with a promise (like a pizza delivery timer)

Potential to build it even bigger

Actionable steps to improve the product or service

Supporting data

Your turn: Instructions

Fill in the sections on the opposite page as follows:

- **WHAT WE THOUGHT, WHAT WE DID, WHAT WE LEARNED SUMMARY.** Describe your progress to date in the test-and-learn phase using this three-part construct.

- **SIGNIFICANT VERBATIMS & OBSERVATIONS.** List critical qualitative information, including customer verbatims from discovery interviews and user input.

- **VALUE DRIVERS & ECONOMIC POTENTIAL.** Summarize information related to revenue potential, pricing, size of market, and economic data.

- **FUTURE SPARK.** Provide a crisp summary of how the initiative maps with trends based on feedback from the customers during the experiment stage.

- **BOOK OF FACTS.** Provide links to supporting evidence, relevant resources, quantitative experiment results, and research references.

- **WHAT TO DO NEXT.** Provide the next step in the validation process. Update this box throughout the process.

BUILD | TOOL
EXPERIMENT TRACKER

EXPERIMENT SUMMARY

WHAT WE THOUGHT
-

WHAT WE DID
-

WHAT WE LEARNED
-

⌄

INSIGHTS & OUTPUTS

SIGNIFICANT VERBATIMS & OBSERVATIONS
-

VALUE DRIVERS & ECONOMIC POTENTIAL
-

FUTURE SPARK
-

BOOK OF FACTS
-

⌄

WHAT TO DO NEXT

NOTES

Key takeaway

The big idea behind the Experiment Tracker tool is to provide a structured and disciplined approach to documenting, assessing, and synthesizing insights from test-and-learn experiments. This tool promotes a collaborative and systematic process for learning from experiments and applying those learnings to drive innovation and decision-making in various business contexts, including internal initiatives, business strategy, co-creation efforts, and complex innovation projects. It emphasizes the importance of aligning the team on what has been learned and using that knowledge to inform future actions and strategies.

What to do next

This model can be applied broadly, including the leadership of internal initiatives, driving a line of business on a new path, spearheading a co-creation initiative, and even complex, multi-year innovation projects. Next, don't forget to pressure test it with the Experiment Pressure Tester.

RESOURCE: EXPERIMENT PRESSURE TESTER CHECKLIST

 Purpose

Guide team sessions.

 How to use it

This is a set of questions designed to guide your evaluation of progress during the Build stage. Meet with your teams to review experiments and pick the most relevant questions. For example, if you're exploring new territory (like Intergráficas did with 3D printing), your team would benefit from a Domain Expertise Perspective. You can then recommend a pause for them to call in a 3D printing expert. If you're experiencing groupthink, look at Innovation Expansion. Who might you co-create with to accelerate progress with your pilot?

Instructions

Schedule review sessions at regular intervals throughout the Build process. Assign one person to lead the team through questions selected from the list to inspire richer evaluation of progress. An outside review panel can also use the Experiment Pressure Tester to structure feedback sessions. It's not necessary to ask all of the questions; pick the ones that are most relevant to your Build project.

BUILD | TOOL
EXPERIMENT PRESSURE TESTER CHECKLIST

- [ ] **VALIDATION/INVALIDATION ASSESSMENT:** Is your team determined?

- [ ] **PIVOT INDICATORS AND IDEAS:** When is it time to change course?

- [ ] **BIAS PRESSURE TESTING:** Are you working with a coach as a check?

- [ ] **PATTERN RECOGNITION:** Do you know which concepts repeat in interviews?

- [ ] **DATA EVALUATION:** Do you know what story the data is telling?

- [ ] **DOMAIN EXPERTISE PERSPECTIVE:** Are you engaging a subject expert?

- [ ] **CROSS-INDUSTRY PERSPECTIVE:** Have you talked with leaders of other industries with expertise you could apply?

- [ ] **EXPERIMENT ANALYSIS:** What other conclusions can you make?

- [ ] **UNTAPPED MARKET INDICATORS:** Do you know where the pent-up demand is?

- [ ] **LONG-TAIL INSIGHTS:** Are you seeing early signs of customer preference?

- [ ] **LIAR'S BOX TESTING:** Where might an interview be inconsistent with a market test result?

- [ ] **BLINDSIDE AWARENESS:** What might you be missing? Who can help you test assumptions?

- [ ] **SCIENTIFIC METHOD DISCIPLINE:** Do you know someone who can check your work?

- [ ] **INSIGHTS ON FORCES THAT COULD DRIVE CHANGE:** Are you tracking new trends and technologies?

- [ ] **MINDSET EXPANSION:** What would have to be true for your new concept to gain traction?

- [ ] **HEADWIND + TAILWIND PERSPECTIVE:** Which competitive or market forces are working in your favor? Against you?

- [ ] **TECHNOLOGY EXPANSION:** Do you know how you could advance your technology capacity?

- [ ] **BUSINESS MODEL EXPANSION:** Is it time to change business models, distribution, logistics, revenue model?

- [ ] **INNOVATION EXPANSION:** Do you know who you can work with or co-create with to accelerate progress?

NOTES

Key takeaway

Use this as a reference for experiment review during the Build stage.

What to do next

Interview end users, potential collaborators, influencers, and other experts using the Uncover Opportunities tool.

TOOL: UNTAPPED OPPORTUNITIES

 Purpose

This tool will help you uncover latent needs or unmet requirements by documenting qualitative interviews that are designed to describe the value of your initiative from the perspective of people who would buy it.

 How to use it + example

Conduct a series of interviews that allow for open-ended responses. The interview teams should consist of at least two people: one person to lead the questioning, and the other to observe and take notes. Ideally, record and transcribe the interviews (with permission). Evaluate the hidden truths. Probe with phrases like "Tell me more."

As compared with a survey or an interview based on a standard questionnaire, these conversations are designed to put the interviewee into a state where they are thinking out loud and sharing impressions. The unmet needs rise to the surface through the open-ended framework.

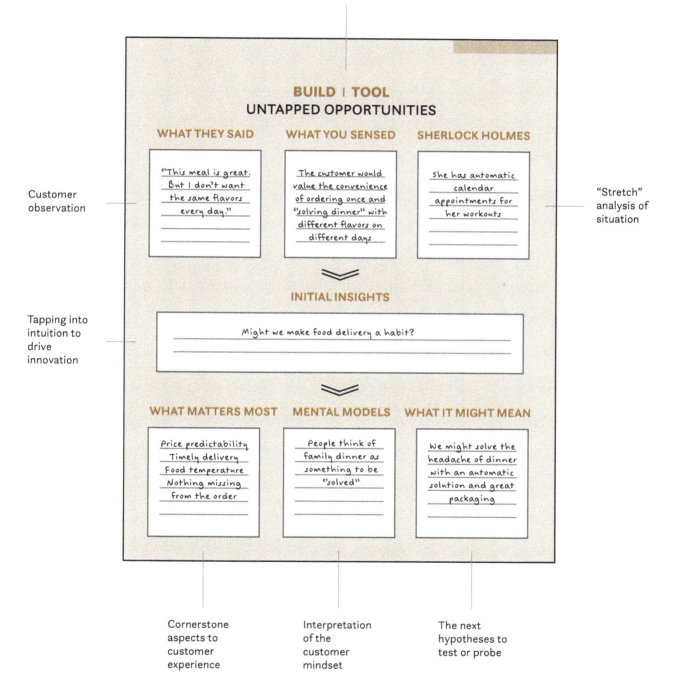

Analysis of
customer
experience

BUILD | TOOL
UNTAPPED OPPORTUNITIES

WHAT THEY SAID

"This meal is great.
But I don't want
the same flavors
every day."

WHAT YOU SENSED

The customer would
value the convenience
of ordering once and
"solving dinner" with
different flavors on
different days

SHERLOCK HOLMES

She has automatic
calendar
appointments for
her workouts

Customer
observation

"Stretch"
analysis of
situation

INITIAL INSIGHTS

Might we make food delivery a habit?

Tapping into
intuition to
drive
innovation

WHAT MATTERS MOST

Price predictability
Timely delivery
Food temperature
Nothing missing
from the order

MENTAL MODELS

People think of
family dinner as
something to be
"solved"

WHAT IT MIGHT MEAN

We might solve the
headache of dinner
with an automatic
solution and great
packaging

Cornerstone
aspects to
customer
experience

Interpretation
of the
customer
mindset

The next
hypotheses to
test or probe

Your turn: Instructions

Fill in the sections on the opposite page as follows:

- **WHAT THEY SAID.** Write down verbatim quotes from the interviews

- **WHAT YOU SENSED.** Jot down some initial impressions of where the customer might be comfortable, confused, or uncomfortable

- **SHERLOCK HOLMES.** Read between the lines. What was the customer trying to tell you? For example, they might be intimidated by new technologies.

- **INITIAL INSIGHTS.** Write down other insights. For example, the person you spoke with might not be the decision maker.

- **WHAT MATTERS MOST.** Which themes kept coming up throughout the conversation? Safety? Security?

- **MENTAL MODELS.** Stepping back from the interview, what categories did the customer seem to have in place already? For example, "Your product sounded like a lot of red tape would be involved."

- **WHAT IT MIGHT MEAN.** Write down the implications for your initiative. For example, "simplify our payment process."

BUILD | TOOL
UNTAPPED OPPORTUNITIES

WHAT THEY SAID

WHAT YOU SENSED

SHERLOCK HOLMES

INITIAL INSIGHTS

WHAT MATTERS MOST

MENTAL MODELS

WHAT IT MIGHT MEAN

NOTES

Key takeaway

Interviews designed to uncover untapped needs are very different from sales conversations or surveys. It takes experience to become skilled at the technique, so start by practicing with people you know. Conduct at least ten to twenty-five interviews to explore a hypothesis.

What to do next

Frame a set of structured strategic sessions that integrate test-and-learn insights that you've uncovered so far. Evaluate your assumptions using the Bias and Blind Spot Tracker later in this module.

TOOL: SCALE OPTIMIZER CHECKLIST

Take a fresh look at your plans for progress, growth, and impact. Don't assume that initiatives that are successful in their early stages will automatically thrive and scale. There are more powerful ways to build significant traction.

 Purpose

Gather circles of supporters, circles of challengers, and circles of strangers to help you explore opportunities to build momentum for your pilot.

 How to use it

Don't think incrementally. Make sure some conversations are designed as future-back scenarios, where you articulate a big challenge and work backward. Other conversations can reveal hidden tripwires to unlock new customer groups or collaborators. You can intentionally orchestrate a true network effect within a new ecosystem. Make sure you're not assuming that your jet ski idea will automatically become a significant ocean liner.

This approach allows us to take a fresh approach to sustainable growth and impact. Growth conversations should happen multiple times in the process.

Sessions that are dedicated to opportunities for growth and scale require a distinct mindset and approach. Don't start them with a traditional SWOT framing or an extension of your current revenue streams and today's workflows. Bring this fresh discipline to uncover new ways to add and capture value.

Here are prompts to structure conversations about how to optimize your new initiative for scale to make sure you are planning beyond the pilot.

SCALE OPTIMIZER CHECKLIST

- [ ] **PLATFORM PLAY:** Could we create a backbone that allows for interoperability?

- [ ] **TECHNOLOGY COMING OF AGE:** Is there an emerging tech (AI, sensors) we could apply?

- [ ] **CAPITAL INFUSION:** Is now the time to infuse an investment to get us ahead faster?

- [ ] **NETWORK EFFECT:** How might growth come through combinatorial forces we help orchestrate?

- [ ] **OPERATIONAL ESCAPE VELOCITY:** Is it time to put a full press of effort from our organization?

- [ ] **SOCIETAL ISSUE OR REGULATORY SHIFT:** Pandemics taught us that we can go fast and big when a shift occurs.

- [ ] **JET SKI OR OCEAN LINER:** Are we waiting for magical scaling from our pilot? How should we shore up to go big?

- [ ] **EXPERIMENT ANALYSIS:** What other conclusions can you make?

- [ ] **THE FUTURE MIGHT BE A JUMP-CUT:** Start with future-back thinking instead of incremental thinking.

- [ ] **RATE LIMITING FACTOR:** Which bottleneck or factor should you focus on eliminating right now?

- [ ] **LABORATORY TRUTH VS. MARKET TRUTH:** Where are your leverage points for growth?

- [ ] **AGENCY OVER THE FUTURE:** Are you missing a chance to "create" a new ecosystem (like electric vehicles)?

NOTES

Key takeaway

Significant growth doesn't happen automatically by taking slow, incremental steps. Forces seem to come out of nowhere, bringing headwinds to our efforts. Laboratory experiments won't grow into full-fledged lines of business without a game plan. We don't automatically blitz-scale growth just because we have a compelling new technology, business model, or customer offering.

What to do next

Conduct a series of sessions with circles of supporters, circles of challengers, and circles of strangers to unlock growth potential. Then, synthesize insights into a set of scenarios that are specifically designed to tackle growth. Link this work to the Ecosystem Mapping in the next module to expand your thinking even more dramatically.

CASE IN POINT
DINA SHERIF, EXECUTIVE DIRECTOR, MIT CENTER FOR DEVELOPMENT AND ENTREPRENEURSHIP

How do you go From Stuck to Scale *in markets where there's no predictability and high volatility?*

Scale—a global, more nuanced perspective

The last thing that business innovators need is a cookie-cutter approach to growth, as if there's a magic formula that will drive businesses' success. In reality, business is a lot more nuanced: unexpected, unprecedented forces can arise.

In some geographies, there's some relative predictability. In others, like in Egypt where I'm from, people have to deal with currency instability. For the markets we serve in our fellow program at MIT that represent growth markets like Africa, Southeast Asia and Latin America, business leaders face constant regulatory shifts.

In markets with a tremendous need for infrastructure, that need to develop leapfrog technologies and where people face complex governmental and geopolitical forces, what's the most appropriate way to define "scale"? How do we look at scale with greater nuance than simply top-line growth? Is becoming a "unicorn" the only end game for entrepreneurs and innovators? These questions are especially important in economies where being a small business owner is often a necessity for providing basic needs like water, food, education, and energy, and to offer a livelihood for families.

In that context, my definition of a successful venture comes down to whether the business is solving complex challenges, whether or not it has the potential to scale and create jobs and generate economic safety or perhaps even wealth.

Having a billion-dollar valuation is not the only prize. Alternative prizes include being able to apply technology and innovation to improve things within the entrepreneur's country, to make their communities better, and to serve an actual need at scale.

Really, the metric that truly matters is how far we have come compared to where we began.

TOOL: BIAS AND BLIND SPOT TRACKER

 Purpose

Use this tool to ensure that your conversations cover all aspects of your initiative or product, ultimately leading to a value proposition that resonates with your target audience. As you continue to refine your ideas and conduct experiments, this tool will be invaluable in your journey toward successful innovation.

 How to use it + example

Apply *From Stuck to Scale*'s four-quadrant thinking to reveal areas where your test-and-learn experiments might be missing a critical area of consideration.

Invite a diverse group to meet with your team to review your experiments, assumptions, and conclusions. Systematically address concerns representing every quadrant of the tool: Engage, Big Picture, Logistics, and Data + Tech.

When the team gets together to reflect on the output of these conversations, it's important to make sure they cover multiple aspects of the initiative or proposed product or service offering.

Examples of the types of sketches you might work on could be an innovative product or service design, an internal transformation within your own company, an ecosystem strategy, or a collaboration designed to bring a co-creation opportunity to market.

BUILD | TOOL
BIASES & BLIND SPOT TRACKER

1. ENGAGEMENT

- Happy ears
- Liar's box
- It's not that
- Selling versus listening
- Doing versus telling

2. BROADER THINKING

- Forces that could drive change
- Cultural lens
- Diversity tone deafness
- Sensemaking
- Combinatorial potential

3. LOGISTICS

- Rigid scaffolding
- Anchoring bias
- Industry norms
- Anomalies
- What would have to be true...

4. DATA & TECH

- Precise data = false security
- Assumption that today's capabilities will transfer
- Industry norm mental model
- Pattern recognition

Spotting incorrect assumptions

Biases related to operations

How analytical information might reveal blind spots

Checking for narrowmindedness

Your turn: Instructions

Fill in the sections on the opposite page as follows:

- **ENGAGEMENT.** Where might you be missing critical customer signals?

- **BROADER THINKING.** Which emerging trends might come into play?

- **LOGISTICS.** How might your go-to-market processes need to shift to roll out your initiative?

- **DATA + TECH.** How might you miss the mark because of an emerging new technology?

Make sure to get multiple insights on where you need to question assumptions.

BUILD | TOOL
BIASES & BLIND SPOT
TRACKER

1. ENGAGEMENT

-
-
-

2. BROADER THINKING

-
-
-

3. LOGISTICS

-
-
-

4. DATA & TECH

-
-
-

NOTES

Key takeaway

It's not just about spotting biases; it's about actively mitigating them to drive innovation and market resonance.

What to do next

Meet with your team. Reflect on all of the activities and insights from the Build module. Continue to do cycles of experiments until you land on a value proposition that resonates with the market. Prepare for the next step, where you will spread your reach to a broader ecosystem: Engage.

CASE IN POINT
ANGELA ROSENQUIST, CHIEF GROWTH OFFICER, INNOVASIAN

Say "no" with confidence:
When to pull the plug

You can feel the energy of a winning team in how they show up to meetings: with fierce determination and commitment to their customers. That's the buzz I felt when I walked into a strategy session with Joe Kent, Dan Peach, and Angela Rosenquist from InnovAsian. At the time, they were a food company with more than $200 million in revenue, and they were committed to growth.

The first-round decision was to expand their brand from Asian-only to a more global set of flavors. For months, they tackled the challenge of how to earn customers in a new flavor segment by applying their expertise in family meals with an Asian theme (like General Tso's chicken) to Latin dishes like adobo rice. What would it take to repurpose their core ingredients like rice and chicken and create recipes that people loved?

The core team rallied the company and went all-in on Latin. For months, they coordinated their test kitchen, customer sessions, pricing models, supply chain, production technologies, and brand team. Every time I visited their Seattle headquarters, I tasted new dishes, saw packaging updates, heard about customer insights, and met with team members who were genuinely excited about the expansion.

This was a can-do company, and their early traction in the market showed that the gung-ho spirit and business savvy was paying off. Clearly, they were a team that had made the right moves toward scaling.

A year or so later, the team considered another path to growth. What if they shifted from family-sized to single-serve-sized packaging? Weren't there customers who ate alone at lunchtime and might want a smaller portion option? Or nights when they wanted to grab a quick meal without the whole family at the table?

Angela was put in charge, and led a rigorous process. She started with a team meeting to gather perspectives on what would make the single-serve project a success. Having just gone through the Latin project, Angela brought forward thinking in all four quadrants from the Bias and Blind Spot Tracker:

- **Engagement.** Whose buy-in mattered most?

- **Broader Thinking.** How could they be best-in-class in single-serve?

- **Logistics.** How might they earn shelf space for a smaller portion size?

- **Data + Tech.** Would single-serve products cannibalize family-sized sales?

Make sure the juice is worth the squeeze

The company knew the drill. They were experienced in doubling down on growth initiatives, and everyone sprang into action. Within a few weeks, they brought forward test kitchen samples, packaging, pricing, supply chain insights, and customer feedback. The momentum was infectious. Everyone was busy trying to make single-serve work. It felt just like the Latin rollout.

Until it didn't.

They did a consumer research study, and the numbers told a story that was tepid, at best. There was an argument to be made to push hard to make single-serve happen, but it would require a ton of effort. They had a huddle with Joe Kent and other senior leaders, and the mood was lukewarm.

Meanwhile, the Latin-brand path was going gangbusters. The flavors sizzled. The customers were excited. The company was jazzed about Latin.

That's when Angela stepped back and took a brave stand.

Late one Monday afternoon, she called to cancel our weekly single-serve standup.

"We're pulling the plug on single-serve," she told me.

She had looked at the cost of defocusing the team compared with the marginal payoff, and decided the juice wasn't worth the squeeze. Better to focus on building out Latin without the distraction of the single-serve initiative.

Just because they *could* move in this tempting new direction, didn't mean they *should*.

Angela made the announcement: "Single-serve is a no-go for now. Instead, we're pulling out all the stops for Latin."

The events that followed proved this was exactly the right decision. InnovAsian accelerated its momentum and generated excitement with its customers.

I remember a mentor telling me that the most brilliant decision an innovation leader can make is to kill a darling. Angela killed that single-serve darling and strengthened overall sales because of it.

Today, the company is on a double-digit growth trajectory. The focus on Latin yielded 4x on distribution attainment of year-one projections, blowing the original forecast out of the water.

Sometimes saying no is the best path toward growth.

SPOTLIGHT STORY: AHURA.AI
Bridging the AI Divide

*Beware the one-size-fits-none
innovation pathway*

When I first met Alex Tsado in 2020, he was at a crossroads. He was working at Nvidia, a company whose valuation today is $3.5 trillion, and whose technologies are the backbone for gaming, high-performance computing, and now AI.

Originally from Nigeria, but working in Silicon Valley, Alex was approached to leave his job and join an independent team to form a startup. This new venture wanted to solve a dramatic challenge related to a soon-to-emerge chapter in AI. It was the days just before ChatGPT caught the public's attention, but Alex and the team foresaw a coming crisis they described as "the AI divide." Companies that figured out how to get ahead of the AI wave would advance quickly, but people who couldn't learn the new tools would find their skillsets obsolete and risk becoming unemployed.

To avoid the AI divide, what if people could train to become mental athletes? These would be people who mastered and stayed current with AI tools as an ongoing capability.

For Alex, the first decision was a personal one. Was joining a startup focused on this compelling challenge the right decision? Or should he stay with the mothership, Nvidia?

He wound up taking the entrepreneurial plunge and, together with two other co-founders, formed Ahura.ai.

From day one, the Ahura team began the real-life Build journey. Like most entrepreneurs, while they were designing their product to address the AI divide they had to deal with multiple pressures, including burn rate and investor expectations. But to Alex, despite the risks inherent in being an entrepreneur, it felt like he was part of a dream team. One of the co-founders had been a sales rock star with another tech company. The other co-founder was an AI pioneer, whose research led to Google Translate and who served on the Google AI ethics board. Combined with Alex's experience in AI infrastructure, they were perfectly positioned to build a product. If they succeeded, Ahura's AI solution would help people learn faster, stay relevant in the workplace, and keep their jobs.

Initial product path:
Let's clone the gems

The initial product path started like that of many successful founders, with sketches. The team spent weeks whiteboarding until they had what looked like a great solution to what they believed was the biggest challenge: replicating great teachers.

The logic went as follows: AI is a new discipline. There are not enough experienced teachers to scale training. Let's clone the gems and multiply a company's training capacity.

And off they went, down the path to simulate great AI teaching. They did what they knew well: videotaped many hours of successful teachers and then analyzed what they saw. They learned a lot about what it took to recognize moments when students became confused, when they disengaged, and what it took to help students progress.

To add product features, they applied their deep technology talents. To address data inclusivity, they debated the cost versus benefit of custom-designed data versus reliance on publicly available data to fuel their models. The team captured and automated some of the most sophisticated aspects of teaching.

From the perspective of building a cool product, they were checking tons of boxes. Sadly, they discovered they were chasing the wrong problem.

The turning point: It's not the teaching, it's the learning

A few months in, Alex and his colleagues sat in a series of user groups that led to a significant strategic turning point. What they observed was that people got excited when they used very simple

"We realized we were doing a great job solving the wrong problem. The first mistake we made was assuming our whiteboard solutions would fly, even without talking with people who were in our target group. Then, we realized we'd rejected some of the simple-to-build solutions because they didn't satisfy our love of bells and whistles."

ALEX TSADO, Co-founder, COO, CPO, Ahura.ai

features—what Alex described as "baby AI." It turned out that simple things, done well, like the inclusion of well-positioned chatbots, kept the learners very engaged. The insight? Ahura's product would do great if it could keep students coming back, alert the manager when there were problems, provide a dashboard to keep track of progress, and ultimately integrate into the workday to make it easy for the learner.

Once they recognized the true problem to be solved, Ahura built with the user in mind, optimized for creating a user experience that sped up learning, created a quick-response dashboard, and delivered a system that fit into the typical workflow to encourage people to come back often and keep progressing.

The allure of bells and whistles had to take a back seat to developing a product that would matter to a lot of people for a long time.

Alex points to the power of user immersion as a reality check to pressure test their provocative whiteboarding.

Once the team came to their important insight, they reengineered the Ahura product to serve today's needs and refocused their strategy to build market demand. They now reach small- and medium-sized customers with tailored AI study buddies, and simultaneously work with large corporations like Salesforce and communities like Davos—where they hosted the Ahura AI House—to drive future global adoption of AI.

AT A GLANCE: AHURA.AI

TOPIC	Ahura.ai assembles a team of rock stars to solve an emerging workforce problem which they call "The AI Divide." Translating a customer gap into an AI product risks becoming a "one size fits none" solution.
FROM STUCK TO SCALE STEP	Build
WHERE PEOPLE GOT STUCK	Spending too much time on the whiteboard and not enough time in the field.

HOW THE FROM STUCK TO SCALE APPROACH WORKS BETTER THAN TRADITIONAL STRATEGY

The Bias and Blind Spot Tracker helps you diagnose blockers in four different categories:

Engagement	Do you have truly involved users, customers and collaborators?
Broader Thinking	Have you stepped back to consider new forces?
Logistics	Where are you stuck in your ways?
Data + Tech	Which experts have you brought in to stretch your thinking?

BREAKTHROUGH MOMENT	When Ahura.ai realized they needed to shift from an emphasis on replicating a teacher to an emphasis on keeping the learner engaged. Used a simpler set of AI tools like chatbots and content design enhancement.
IMPACT	• **AI Study Buddy:** Focused product strategy designed to serve small- and medium-sized businesses • **AI capacity-building with corporations** (Salesforce, Spurt) • **Online education** (Wayfinder, Nevada Partners) • **Societal impact** (Conrad Foundation, Carlos Beltran Foundation)
KEY INSIGHT	Just because you can build something complex, doesn't mean you should.
HOW YOU CAN APPLY THIS	Take out the Bias and Blind Spot Tracker. Hold four different sessions to check your assumptions, one focused on each of the four quadrants. Listen and learn.
FINAL TIP	It's tempting to jump to a solution too soon, especially when there's deep product or technology talent on the team. Enforce checkpoints to uncover bias and address blind spots.

CHAPTER SUMMARY

>> Key insights

When things get real, we're tempted to put the brakes on innovation. Our experiments will lead to disappointments, like when Intergráficas realized their future might not be in the music industry. We might accidentally put our finger on the scale to tip the results from a pilot toward a direction we're comfortable with. We'll likely hit the wall when a pet project or favorite technology doesn't pan out as a viable option for the future.

Traditional training suggests we "pivot," but they don't teach us how exactly to do that.

It takes new tools to make sure we don't stay in the muck, can move past blind spots, and scale effectively.

>> Key Stuck Points

STUCK POINTS: FRICTION, RESISTANCE, OBSTACLES, CHALLENGES	TOOL TO USE	HOW IT WORKS
You've brainstormed enough. Now it's time to get real. Can you turn your blue-sky ideas into test-and-learn experiments?	Ideaboard (part 2)	Focuses the team on the aspects of each pilot that could decide the go versus no-go.
Experiments on what's possible land on a manager's desk in the midst of a busy agenda. Can you systematize them?	Experiment Tracker	Applies sprint-like discipline to Build experiments: everyone has a common reporting dashboard and outsiders offer reality checks and ideation.
The key here is finding unmet needs. Can you maintain discipline to reach out to new people to discover a new direction?	Untapped Opportunities	Structures discovery interviews that are key to revealing current market gaps that your team could fill.
If we're not careful, we'll end the Build stage with a bunch of "science fair projects" that can never make it big in the real world. How might you incorporate thinking about scale as part of your experiments?	Scale Optimizer	Engineers growth and bold impact directly into the pilot stage. As teams lead and evaluate experiments that work on a small scale, they simultaneously pressure-test ideas: How could this go big?
We all have happy ears when it comes to the things we're familiar with (music, for example) and blind spots for ideas outside our realms of experience or expertise. How will your team push beyond your blind spots?	Biases and Blind Spot Tracker	Imposes guards against bias. Use this as a filter in evaluation sessions, considering blind spots in four categories. Engagement: Whose input to include in our evaluation? Broader Thinking: Are we missing opportunities to go big? Logistics: Have we inadvertently created unnecessary friction? Data + Tech: Which technologies or new inventions might be applied to create 10x value?

>> Key actions

It's essential to focus on four core areas to make sure we don't hit a wall when we translate our Expand whiteboards into tangible pilots:

1   Apply the rigor of experiments to make our growth ideas real

2   Train ourselves to have a new type of conversation, designed to uncover unmet needs and hidden priorities

3   Invite experts from outside our core business into our experimentation teams

4   Identify and mitigate Biases and Blind Spots

This involves breaking down your initiative into experiments, conducting interviews to open fresh markets to pursue and products to provide, tracking experiment progress, and challenging assumptions.

>> Key question

The key question to address in this chapter is:

"How can we ground our innovative ideas in reality, learn from experiments, and address challenges as we strive to scale our initiatives?"

>> Commitment

To truly advance our initiatives, we commit to continuously refining and validating our ideas through experiments, conducting interviews to understand user needs, tracking our progress diligently, and embracing diverse perspectives to uncover blind spots and biases that may hinder our innovation journey.

It's tempting to race from the whiteboard directly to the accelerator to start building. That's a fatal mistake. The best leaders discover emerging customer needs, technologies, and market conditions before they rush to start building.

STEP 4

ENGAGE
CREATING MAXIMUM VALUE

GOAL: Bring others into the fold:
internal, external, complementary

WHERE MIGHT YOU BE STUCK?

In this chapter, we'll address some of the following Stuck Points—friction, resistance, obstacles, and challenges—that might sound like this:

- "We won awards for our MVP but now can't get the organizational support, budget, and resources we need to build it bigger."

- "We don't know how to bring in partners, collaborators, co-creators to expand."

- "As we start to execute, we drift back into incremental thinking."

- "It's hard to keep up the momentum as we return to day-to-day priorities."

Unsure where your situation fits in?

Visit www.andreakates.com/diagnostic and take the *From Stuck to Scale* Diagnostic to take stock.

Everyone needs
to be a hero in
their own story.

"THERE'S A HUGE difference between great results in the business laboratory and making those results real with employees, suppliers, investors, and customers," Nicolas Cortázar said, expressing the pressure he felt right after the Build stage.

The experiments indicated an opportunity to move Intergráficas away from its heritage as a music CD production house to become a printing and packaging company serving the food industry. On paper, it sounded like a promising way out of the struggle to serve a dying market. But to translate the pilot into reality, Nicolas had to enter his first staff meeting with a game plan for Engage.

First, he had to engage the employees to shift their focus from music to printing. It's not an easy mindset shift for people who have spent their careers following bands and hanging out at festivals. Then, the company had to build a network of new customers in the food industry. Engaging a supply chain for paper would turn out to be complicated as the pandemic hit. Not incidentally, Nicolas needed to garner support for the transformation from his investors.

As Nicolas opened the door to that first staff meeting, he was painfully aware that the room was filled with people whose jobs were on the line if the new direction were to flop. What happened next involved a combination of smart strategy, terrible luck, and, eventually, good fortune.

Nicolas had to set the tone. He resisted the temptation to convince everyone to get on board. He didn't deliver the standard "elevator pitch" that many innovators are coached to do. Instead, he let the pilot team present the data from the experiments, all of which pointed to a solid future in the food industry. He let employees articulate their perspectives on what resonated with them using commitment narratives. The team brought forward ideas to multiply their impact by building customer relationships in the food industry with small food suppliers, restaurants, and national chains.

They polished up their hidden manufacturing gem, a highly efficient and tech-enabled print shop, to get it ready to service the food industry.

They sketched an initial ecosystem map and expanded their perspectives on who they'd need to engage with, from paper suppliers to food safety experts.

In the spirit of true engagement, the team got busy. They set out to meet with everyone on that map, using the Commitment Narrative as a structure for their conversations. They enlisted buy-in from enough customers to begin some in-market rollouts. The operational leads started negotiating with paper suppliers, meeting with the Department of Health and having sessions with packaging designers.

They hit a key milestone when KFC, a national food chain, signed a contract.

The plan achieved commitment from investors, whose concerns about the shrinking market for CDs seemed to be addressed by the shift in strategy. The clock was ticking, though, with cash running short.

Despite the pressure, the company doubled down on its innovation DNA, reimagining how it might become a truly transformative leader in food packaging. They identified and then had sessions with people with creative concepts for sustainable materials and easy-to-deliver food containers.

It seemed as if everything was on track.

Then, the pandemic hit. How would Intergráficas survive if restaurants closed and the workforce had to stay home?

INITIATIVES THAT thrive at a small scale are not guaranteed to maintain momentum. The critical ingredient is engagement—from people, teams, departments, collaborators, partners, investors, customers, and other ecosystem players.

The ideal way to work with the Engage tools is through individual work and team discussions and sessions. You'll progress your initiative from the early version you developed in the Build module through to an initiative with buy-in from a rich ecosystem.

The initiatives you work through can be internal or external. There might be an internal transformation initiative you're considering, a customer-facing concept, a new line of business, an innovative business model, or an ecosystem play.

Your practical toolkit

The process of driving full commitment begins here. Full engagement requires four ingredients, which are at the heart of gaining commitment, expanding participation, and extending our reach.

In this chapter, we have four canvases.

Commitment Narratives

Summarizes the perspectives of critical stakeholders concerning your initiative. The critical lesson is that each individual's reason for supporting your initiative might be distinct. The key is to understand what matters to them and to uncover their perspectives on the impact your initiative might bring.

Impact Multiplier

Outlines specific ways to tap into the opportunity to build your initiative bigger. The multiplier effect from your initiative could come from combinations of forces that drive growth.

Let's dive in so you can learn more about your team's commitment narratives.

Ecosystem Mapper

Engineers significant scale and impact into a new initiative. Traditional thinking about ecosystems didn't take true advantage of the multiplier potential of interconnected players whose efforts are orchestrated to bring value to everyone. Leaders today can apply more advanced ecosystem thinking to drive profit or attract people to an interoperable common platform and ultimately achieve a game-changing impact through an ecosystem of purpose.

Transformative Leadership

Articulates how we might amplify our impact. As leaders, we can position our initiatives at various levels of impact. We might set our sights on incremental improvements with strong value, or stretch our ambitions to drive an entirely new market direction or address a major societal challenge.

TOOL: COMMITMENT NARRATIVES

 ## Purpose

To articulate motivating factors for each person in the ecosystem. Address the common misconception that everyone advancing a new initiative should be doing it for the same reasons. Truth: getting to each person's "why" unlocks their willingness to participate and can ignite excitement, urgency, and buy-in.

 ## How to use it + example

Do not guess, interview! Conduct at least five to ten interviews with people representing each category. Reflect on how they view your project's potential, and write out the narrative, value, future potential, and impact in their words.

Create a separate Commitment Narrative for every person whose buy-in is key to success.

Focus leaders of initiatives on the need to identify the unique reasons that various people in the ecosystem will be committed to participation. It's critical to understand that it takes various versions of a narrative to resonate with different stakeholders; the discipline of uncovering the "why" behind each party's motivation is the secret to support.

Overview of current state and future ambition told through one lens

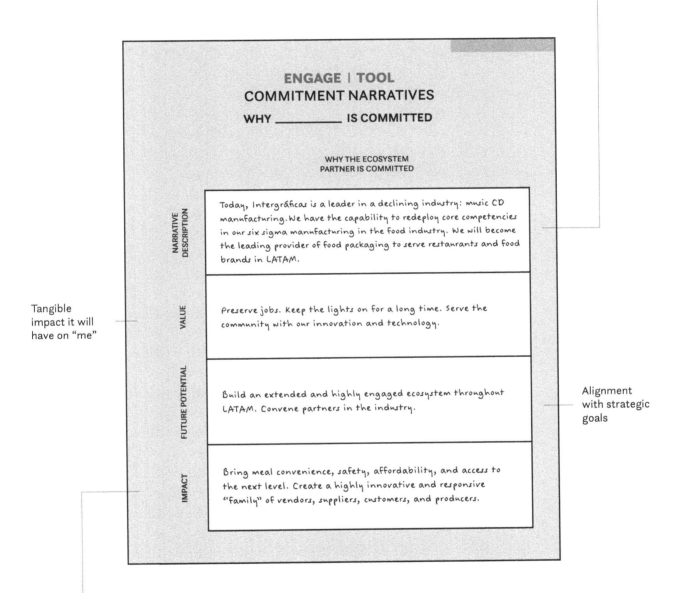

ENGAGE | TOOL
COMMITMENT NARRATIVES
WHY _____ IS COMMITTED

**WHY THE ECOSYSTEM
PARTNER IS COMMITTED**

NARRATIVE DESCRIPTION

Today, Intergráficas is a leader in a declining industry: music CD manufacturing. We have the capability to redeploy core competencies in our six sigma manufacturing in the food industry. We will become the leading provider of food packaging to serve restaurants and food brands in LATAM.

VALUE

Preserve jobs. Keep the lights on for a long time. Serve the community with our innovation and technology.

FUTURE POTENTIAL

Build an extended and highly engaged ecosystem throughout LATAM. Convene partners in the industry.

IMPACT

Bring meal convenience, safety, affordability, and access to the next level. Create a highly innovative and responsive "family" of vendors, suppliers, customers, and producers.

Tangible impact it will have on "me"

Alignment with strategic goals

How "I" will measure future success

Your turn: Instructions

Fill in the sections on the opposite page as follows:

- **NARRATIVE DESCRIPTION.** Instead of trying to create one generic "elevator pitch," meet with the leaders whose commitment, support, and participation will be most important to the success of your initiative. Fill out one column at a time. In every column, fill out a different narrative version using words that resonate with the leader. The form has columns for people inside and outside your organization.

- **VALUE.** What does the person you're talking to care about? How will they measure the value? When you look at all the columns together, how do they help you define priorities?

- **FUTURE POTENTIAL.** Talk with each leader to articulate the potential they see in this new project.

- **IMPACT.** Capture the metrics that each leader considers "impactful." Revenue? Ability to round out a suite of services for critical customers? KPIS? OKRS? Something else?

COMMITMENT NARRATIVES PART ONE

	WHY I AM COMMITTED	WHY THE TEAM IS COMMITTED	WHY THE COMPANY IS COMMITTED
NARRATIVE DESCRIPTION	• •	• •	• •
VALUE	• •	• •	• •
FUTURE POTENTIAL	• •	• •	• •
IMPACT	• •	• •	• •

COMMITMENT NARRATIVES PART TWO

	WHY THE ECOSYSTEM PARTNER IS COMMITTED	WHY THE CUSTOMER IS COMMITTED	WHY THE COMMUNITY IS COMMITTED
NARRATIVE DESCRIPTION	• •	• •	• •
VALUE	• •	• •	• •
FUTURE POTENTIAL	• •	• •	• •
IMPACT	• •	• •	• •

Key takeaway

These core value drivers can be related to the customer, the market, technology advancement, ecosystem enhancement, or data leverage. The impact could be measured based on operational improvements, contribution to culture, ability to attract talent, growth metrics, profitability measures, or societal impact.

As you activate people in the next phase, connect back to each stakeholder's specific descriptions of perceived value, perspectives on the future potential of the initiative, and point of view about the impact.

What to do next

Widen your lens on commitment. Apply the Impact Multiplier tool to consider big ideas for bringing a significantly larger group of people on board.

TOOL: IMPACT MULTIPLIER

 ## Purpose

This tool is designed to inspire expanded project ambitions based on specific probes for your initiatives.

 ## How to use it + example

Assign teams to research examples in the six categories that could create a combinatorial and interconnected organization that all benefit from the new direction.

Conduct a series of facilitated sessions to identify specific areas where your initiative could grow based on elements identified by the teams.

Combine your thinking about the big picture and action steps to set the course for imagination and implementation.

Opportunities to implement other platforms with product

Innovative technologies to be utilized

ENGAGE | TOOL
IMPACT MULTIPLIER

PLATFORM PLAY
Integration with payments systems?

TECHNOLOGY COMING OF AGE
Gamification and habit creation for families ordering meals. Might we mine big data to know our customers better?

CAPITAL INFUSION
Might we partner with our customers like KFC to deploy a backend solution?

NETWORK EFFECT
How might we replicate KFC to serve other large clients?

OPERATIONAL ESCAPE VELOCITY
Might we become the infrastructure partner for marketing, promotion, as well as packaging?

SOCIETAL ISSUE / REGULATORY SHIFT
Safe food, every day, that's convenient and affordable. Eco-friendly and sustainable. Plastic reduction.

Opportunities for raising money from key stakeholders

Ways to gain massive product traction

Shifts in larger scale trends to harness

Ways to amplify growth through partner dynamics

Your turn: Instructions

Fill in the sections on the opposite page as follows:

- **PLATFORM PLAY.** How might you tap into an existing platform to serve an entirely new set of customers?

- **TECHNOLOGY COMING OF AGE.** How might you tap into a new technology to leapfrog into a new market?

- **CAPITAL INFUSION.** Might your new initiative unlock a significant capital investment from a partner or a customer group?

- **NETWORK EFFECT.** How might your new business model leverage your company into an interconnected set of new relationships?

- **OPERATIONAL ESCAPE VELOCITY.** How might you focus on building infrastructure that supports significant growth?

- **SOCIETAL ISSUE / REGULATOR SHIFT.** How might you tap into a new requirement (for example, fintech authentication and government compliance) to become a preferred provider?

IMPACT MULTIPLIER

PLATFORM PLAY

TECHNOLOGY COMING OF AGE

CAPITAL INFUSION

NETWORK EFFECT

OPERATIONAL ESCAPE VELOCITY

SOCIETAL ISSUE / REGULATORY SHIFT

NOTES

Key takeaway

The only way to escape from incrementalism is to jolt ourselves into fresh approaches to growth. Intergráficas paved the way for a game change by building a scalable infrastructure at the same time they tested food concepts at a pilot scale. That strategy opened the door for a shift in their ecosystem from the music industry to the food industry. Pilots gain escape velocity when scale is planned for from the start.

What to do next

Work in teams to develop detailed research, learning, and mastery work streams to expand your expertise in each strategic arena. Identify startups, collaborators, partners, or experts who can help you establish relationships to fuel ecosystem expansion. Then, use the Ecosystem Mapper to design your ecosystem game plan.

TOOL: ECOSYSTEM MAPPER

 ## Purpose

Map the community of interconnected parts and players whose contribution and participation will multiply impact. This tool addresses the combinatorial impact that can be achieved when your strategy begins with a future perspective on the ecosystem that could bring scale to your initiative and the forces allowing multiple parties to bring value and succeed.

 ## How to use it + example

Begin with the partners in your immediate line of sight: vendors, customers, suppliers. Then, add additional categories and players whose participation could accelerate progress.

Consider ecosystems designed to help drive profit (or, if you are a government or non-profit organization, drive membership or build a constituency) and ecosystems that organize multiple parties on an interoperable platform.

Expand your map to include players whose participation could work to achieve objectives representing a higher purpose collectively. Examples include transitioning from hospital-based care to home care and establishing a new mobility infrastructure.

Ask questions like:

- How might we drive new value into the equation?

- How might existing relationships evolve in a newly configured ecosystem?

- Which models might bring breakthroughs?

- Which forces might be at play that we should consider (e.g., regulatory, geopolitical)?

- Where might we have agency over a bigger future?

- Who might be important parties with whom to establish relationships now?

Diagram of
most effective
way to make
money

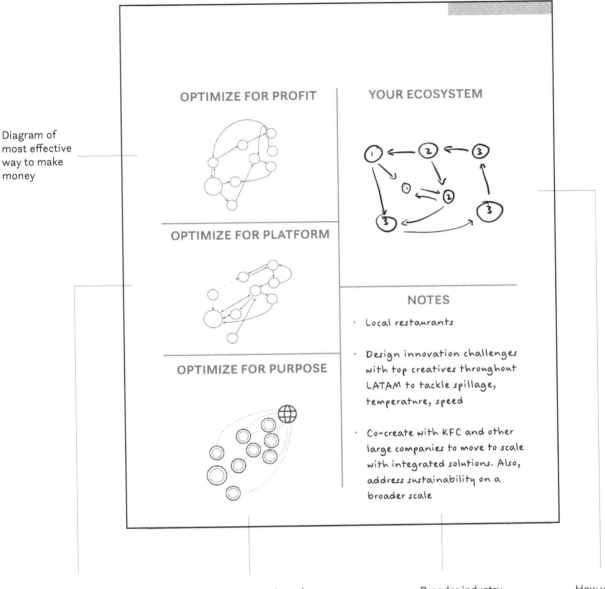

OPTIMIZE FOR PROFIT

YOUR ECOSYSTEM

OPTIMIZE FOR PLATFORM

NOTES

· Local restaurants

· Design innovation challenges
with top creatives throughout
LATAM to tackle spillage,
temperature, speed

· Co-create with KFC and other
large companies to move to scale
with integrated solutions. Also,
address sustainability on a
broader scale

OPTIMIZE FOR PURPOSE

Focus on
frictionless
processes and
interoperability

Impact as viewed
from a richer
perspective

Broader industry
notes and
observations

How you'd
structure the
optimal
ecosystem

Fill in the sections on the opposite page
as follows:

- **OPTIMIZE FOR PROFIT.** Use the drawing in
  the top-left square to label your initial ecosystem map optimized for "profit." Put your
  own company in the center of the drawing
  and label the supply chain and partners
  who could help grow revenues for your new
  initiative while they grow their revenues.

- **OPTIMIZE FOR PLATFORM.** In the middle-left
  square, think about the interoperability of
  multiple parties through a platform. Label
  the ecosystem for your new initiative if you
  optimized for frictionless interactions.

- **OPTIMIZE FOR PURPOSE.** Does your
  initiative have the potential to optimize
  for "purpose?" Label the circles in the
  bottom-left square with purpose-based
  opportunities.

- **YOUR ECOSYSTEM.** Brainstorm with your
  team to draw your ideal ecosystem from
  scratch, considering profit, platform, and
  purpose as well as other important perspectives and success metrics.

- **NOTES.** Capture notes from the brainstorming session to explain your ecosystem map.

ENGAGE | TOOL
ECOSYSTEMS MAPPER

OPTIMIZE FOR PROFIT

YOUR ECOSYSTEM

OPTIMIZE FOR PLATFORM

NOTES

-
-
-

OPTIMIZE FOR PURPOSE

NOTES

Key takeaway

Ecosystem Mapping is a perfect process for collaboration and co-creation. Convene teams representing different interests, perspectives, and points of view for dynamic co-creation. Apply technology tools for mapping such as an AI-enabled search for expansion of key categories, and scenario thinking to evolve the map.

What to do next

Based on your expanded thinking about ecosystems, stretch your overall ambitions for the impact you will create using the Transformative Leadership tool.

If you've drawn your ecosystem with YOUR company as the biggest, most central circle on the map, it's not an ecosystem, it's an ego-system.

CASE IN POINT
FRANK BONAFILIA, COFOUNDER
THE EDISON AWARDS AND LEWIS
LATIMER FELLOWS

The only way to solve big challenges: lead ecosystems that drive shared value and collective purpose

Focus on sustainability and circularity
Whenever Frank calls, I answer immediately. Frank Bonafilia, Executive Director of the Edison Awards, was inviting me to be part of their Meet the Innovator forum. Named for Thomas Edison, the community spotlights the best inventions, technologies, and innovative products. They have honored leaders like Jonny Ive and established the Lewis Latimer Fellows.

The topic Frank wanted to focus on: How could the Edison community inspire its members to make bold moves?

The solution? Highlight the role of ecosystems as a force multiplier for innovation.

I set out to discover who was pushing the boundaries and taking on the wicked problems that require expertise from different disciplines.

In conversation after conversation with leaders from the Edison community, I heard firsthand accounts from corporations that apply ecosystems to achieve breakthroughs, and was most impressed with the experiences at Cargill and SABIC. In both cases, the leaders led grand challenges with science, technology, and research at the core.

Our session at the Meet the Innovator forum spotlighted the leaders of those initiatives: Florian Schattenmann, CTO and VP of R&D and Innovation at Cargill, and Dr. Bob Maughon, Executive Vice President Sustainability, Technology & Innovation

and Chief Technology and Sustainability Officer at SABIC. Here are highlights from our conversation.

One of Cargill's powers is being a great connector. This gives us a unique opportunity and responsibility to act. We work with academics, startups, governments, and of course our customers—from farmers to food service operators to CPGS—creating solutions that build a better future. This ecosystem approach allows players to connect to carbon markets, collaborate on science, and connect dots to solve some of our industry's biggest challenges. Innovation is the ultimate team sport!

At the same time, inside our four walls, our R&D programs keep pushing the limits, opening the door for altogether new innovations that are better for our health, environment, and people.

We have deep roots and rich capabilities in regenerative agriculture, built in support of our purpose to nourish the world in a safe, responsible, sustainable way. For example, the underlying science related to the sweetener Stevia has led to real environmental benefits while delivering a natural, low-calorie sweetener that consumers are looking for.

Because we discovered that the sweetness of Stevia could be produced through fermentation instead of the traditional soil-based growing methods, we explored an entirely new approach to our sustainability goals.

Innovative discovery combined with an investment in ecosystem collaboration accelerates our ability to scale.

We're at a pivotal moment when metrics like NPV and other financial metrics as the leading measure of success need to take a back seat. To truly solve the next wave of challenges, like sustainability, circularity, and large-scale innovation, we need a new structure for problem solving.

What we've done at SABIC is drive ecosystem-level collaboration, which has required us to rethink the concept of risk. We've also driven collaboration with partners who have been our competition in the past.

Painting the picture for the chemical industry: eighty percent of our emissions come from heat. That makes decarbonization a complex topic. When we stepped back, we recognized that the ideal partner to work on decarbonization with us was Linde Engineering, whose furnace-related technologies allowed us to decarbonize

"Push the limits. Expand the ecosystem."

FLORIAN SCHATTENMANN

"We can't afford to wait for everything to be de-risked before we innovate."

BOB MAUGHON

our assets. That posed a strategic problem—Linde's partner, BASF, is a competitor in parts of the market, so if we'd applied a traditional mindset, we might have considered brainstorming with them to be a strategic risk.

But, with the mindset of solving a critical problem, we realized that their tech-savviness was our best path toward a game-changing solution.

Our team shifted away from viewing other companies simply as customers, suppliers, or competitors. It was clear that we needed to innovate and collaborate in ways we're not used to doing, by forming collaborative ecosystem relationships where SABIC plays the role of facilitator.

By abandoning siloed thinking and adopting a broader perspective on competition, we've made significant strides toward our sustainability objectives.

When we know we need a breakthrough, what's the best way to tackle wicked challenges? Gather diverse disciplines and lead an ecosystem.

TOOL: TRANSFORMATIVE LEADERSHIP

 ### Purpose

This tool opens the possibilities for multiple ways to achieve greater impact and engage new people.

Elevate your level of ambition from a basic improvement toward a higher-impact opportunity. Fuel buy-in from groups of constituents, co-creators, partners, and peers by including them in the process to build bolder solutions.

 ### How to use it + example

Work as a group to build bolder, bigger concepts. Begin by distilling your perspective on how to drive bolder impact through your new initiative. Then, start at the bottom left and articulate how you might improve today, redesign tomorrow, reimagine the future, and ultimately lead the future (the first column). Generate many ideas for each box (don't be limited by the space on the sample form).

Then, for each idea, brainstorm ideas for the second (Who) and third (How) columns.

Opportunities for
game-changing
potential

ENGAGE | TOOL
TRANSFORMATIVE LEADERSHIP

	FOCUS AREA	WHO	HOW
LEAD THE FUTURE	Sustainable farm-to-table ecosystem, eco-friendly materials	Agtech leaders, university research	Convene conferences, invent new materials
REIMAGINE THE FUTURE	Affordable meals for everyone, daily	Local food banks, government	Embrace multiple price points and delivery modes
REDESIGN TOMORROW	Co-create with KFC. Create a community of customers	KFC, local restaurants, startup accelerators	Establish an innovation lab
IMPROVE TODAY	Make meal delivery safe and convenient for LATAM families	App developers, health inspectors, community leaders	Integrate with apps, master health standards

Creative
ambitions for
innovation

Novel
business
models to
improve
customer
experience

Make today's
business
model better

Your turn: Instructions

Fill in the sections on the opposite page as follows:

- **LEAD THE FUTURE.** Stretch your ambitions. How might your project become a movement, lead your industry, expand globally, or otherwise Lead the Future?

- **REIMAGINE THE FUTURE.** How might you think ahead and leapfrog your project? For example, a bank might collaborate with startups to create seamless cross-border payments.

- **REDESIGN TOMORROW.** Which coming trend can you integrate into your project? Can you apply new technology? Serve a new customer group or an adjacent market?

- **IMPROVE TODAY.** How will your project improve your customers' lives or add value to your existing ecosystem?

- **FOCUS AREA.** Determine the emphasis for your innovation. Examples: technology, customer experience, process.

- **WHO.** Identify a partner or person who might help bring this idea forward with you.

- **HOW.** Jot down a quick thought of how you might take a first step.

TRANSFORMATIVE LEADERSHIP

	FOCUS AREA	WHO	HOW
LEAD THE FUTURE			
REIMAGINE THE FUTURE			
REDESIGN TOMORROW			
IMPROVE TODAY			

NOTES

Key takeaway

Leaders face a spectrum of options once they begin the *From Stuck to Scale* process. At the most basic level, they can make a transactional and incremental change, or they can lead a larger initiative. The impetus for going bolder could be because the need is so strong (like the home healthcare demand) or because success at a small scale inspires the team to enlist more partners and create a true transformation ecosystem. No matter which impact is achieved in the first implementation phase, the team can always revisit this exercise to ask, "How might we build this bolder and achieve greater impact?"

What to do next

Synthesize your insights and imagine the ecosystem that might serve or be served by your bolder view of what could lie ahead.

SPOTLIGHT STORY: MAYO CLINIC
Gold Mine or Landmine?

*Overcoming resistance to bring a
life-saving technology to market*

The first time I met James (Jim) Rogers many years ago, we discovered that we had intersecting business interests. He was seeking solutions to bring medical and scientific discoveries to market. The level of scrutiny for this activity was high since Jim worked at Mayo Clinic, a world leader in healthcare. I was running a software company that was the backbone for the discipline used by the National Science Foundation, working with large and innovative companies like Intel and Nasdaq to commercialize early-stage ideas and bring them to scale.

That initial meeting with Jim spotlighted the role of Mayo Clinic Ventures, a core group within Mayo Clinic's Department of Business Development that focuses on matching the organization's intellectual property with product-market fit to coincide with customer, patient, and healthcare practitioner needs. The team is charged with advancing novel ideas with spectacular discipline, ranging from digital consumer health wearables to cutting-edge diagnostics.

A leader of this group, Jim and his team have helped shepherd a myriad of technologies and collaborative efforts that have resulted in tremendous impact, including innovative, patient-centered responses to COVID-19 and responsibility for AI applications. The range of challenges can be considerable, but the consistent ability to get beyond stuck and move initiatives to scale compels action. The story of Mayo Clinic and Exact Sciences highlights one use case.

Have you ever experienced frustration when a promising initiative can't get the support it needs to move from incubation to market rollout?

Leaders who have nurtured pilots and successfully defined strong business models often believe clear wins in the Build stage should automatically be given the resources needed to reach more people without resistance. The unfortunate truth is that we've all experienced that "gotcha" moment when pushback appears, either tapping the brakes on progress or, worse, shutting down a new line of business altogether.

That's exactly where Mayo Clinic found itself when it landed the opportunity to advance what would later turn out to be a life-saving technology that almost failed the Engagement hurdle. The steps they took to earn trust and gain commitment provide universal lessons in moving past obstacles and planting seeds for dramatic growth.

Uncovering a new solution for patients

Mayo Clinic operates with an enduring commitment to looking beyond today's horizon in order to pinpoint new solutions to save more lives. On any given day, the organization's thousands of staff members are unearthing and propelling novel solutions to address unmet patient needs.

The genesis of this particular example stems from one Mayo Clinic team's identification of colon cancer as a vital area to tackle, a direction in which health statistics provided ample support: the World Health Organization projected an increase in incidence of sixty-three percent by 2040. Greatly reducing that figure seemed within reach in knowing that early detection

"There are many ways people get stuck. They get personally invested in a specific outcome. They worry about sunk costs. They get so busy in the day-to-day that they can't see strategically. It's up to leaders to push beyond the horizon and, in our case, focus on saving more lives. It's that simple."

JAMES ROGERS, Chief Business Development Officer and Senior Administrator for Generative AI, Mayo Clinic

makes a tremendous difference in health outcomes for colon cancer.

It was evident there was a strong case for increasing the number of people tested to better identify those at risk for cancer early. At-home screening seemed like a hopeful solution.

Following years of research and development in the space, Mayo Clinic had the initial components for the technology, but not what was needed to fully establish it as a test suitable for mass rollout. A powerful consideration then presented itself: Work with an outside partner to finalize the development of the technology as a deployable at-home colorectal cancer screening test, and integrate it into Mayo Clinic's suite of diagnostic offerings.

Skepticism makes its debut

It seemed like a no-brainer: reach more patients by administering the test, refer more cases to Mayo Clinic and save more lives. While a unanimous vote in favor of this initiative would seem to be the likely result, the surprising response it actually elicited underscores universal insights on the importance of Engage as a critical element for bringing an initiative to life.

In contrast to the expectation for broad support, trepidation materialized. An array of questions, based on years of expertise, challenged the proposal at hand:

- Should Mayo Clinic attempt to develop the test itself using its business model for diagnostics, or should the organization invest its resources with a partner to bring it through FDA approval and scale to patients?

- Could an external test, augmented outside Mayo Clinic's walls, match Mayo Clinic's rigid standards?

- Wouldn't an at-home test cannibalize Mayo Clinic's colonoscopy practice?

As illogical as it sounds, projects that are potential gold mines can become landmines, hitting raw nerves inside a company or resistance in the ecosystem of suppliers, vendors, and partners. Uncharted terrain can often generate doubt and apprehension.

Resolution meets scalability

Mayo Clinic Ventures ultimately licensed the technology to Exact Sciences, a molecular diagnostics company, that worked alongside Mayo Clinic's principal investigator and team to further fine-tune and scale the technology, paving way for what would ultimately become the FDA-approved, at-home test widely known today as Cologuard.

This innovative technology set the stage for a future where early detection could become commonplace, showing the possibility of bringing cancer screening efforts to the masses and saving a significant number of lives in the process.

So, what was the magic behind the Engage strategy for landing on this positive conclusion?

First, the involved stakeholders didn't brute-force their way through the objections to the proposal. Instead, they addressed them carefully and precisely, applying the mindset of *From Stuck to Scale*'s Engage toolset. They focused on uncovering what it would take to establish trust in an ecosystem partner and gain commitment in adopting a "not-fully-established-here" technology.

Facts at the foundation

Despite the apprehension voiced, the gavel didn't bang down with a firm "no." The decision makers resisted the temptation to frame the opportunity according to the standard operating procedure and resisted rejection for embracing a new direction. They simply laid out the facts.

This required shifting the focus from proving the technology and validating a new business model—critical elements of the Build stage—toward establishing trust for an outside collaborator and allowing the internal research team's efforts to be built upon in a way that would have the quickest and most impactful outcome.

Widening the net of patients served and expanding Mayo Clinic's role in saving lives was what served as a North Star in determining the verdict.

Use tools like the Commitment Narrative and Ecosystem Mapping to focus on winning over individuals and multiplying the impact of partners.

AT A GLANCE: MAYO CLINIC

SITUATION	Mayo Clinic can collaborate with an outside partner to enhance colon cancer detection and treatment.
FROM STUCK TO SCALE STEP	Engage
WHERE PEOPLE GOT STUCK	After thoughtful exploration, a proposition for a new business model to advance a technology in question that included an outside partner was met with internal resistance.
HOW THE FROM STUCK TO SCALE APPROACH WORKS BETTER THAN THE TRADITIONAL STRATEGY	The Commitment Narrative focuses on what each subset of decision makers cares about. The traditional strategy focuses on a logical model but misses the nuances of "illogical" elements that drive resistance.
BREAKTHROUGH MOMENT	After a rigorous evaluation of the capabilities and robust product development history of Exact Sciences, Mayo Clinic finally concluded that a strategic collaboration made more sense than trying to deploy an at-home test on their own. The shared effort would be the most advantageous for patients.
IMPACT	Cologuard is the first and only test that looks for abnormal blood and DNA in stool, detecting 92% of colon cancers. Mayo Clinic is currently leading a prospective survey-based study[2] with 150,000 participants to gather real-world evidence on Cologuard's impact on long-term outcomes in a large, diverse population. This is the largest[3] prospective, observational colorectal cancer screening study ever conducted.[4]
KEY INSIGHT	Logic isn't the only component that drives commitment.
HOW YOU CAN APPLY THIS	Remember that the reasons people support a new idea are not the same as the forces that come into play when that idea becomes a reality about to go big.
FINAL TIP	Don't assume that you'll get support and resources just because logic is in your favor. Even when people want an idea to move forward based on rational thinking, other dynamics can result in your project getting stuck.

2   https://www.mayo.edu/research/clinical-trials/cls-20467318

3   https://www.prnewswire.com/news-releases/exact-sciences-and-mayo-clinic-initiate-150-000-patient-7-year-study-to-evaluate-real-world-impact-of-cologuard-300937584.html

4   Visit the following link for more information: https://newsnetwork.mayoclinic.org/discussion/clinical-trials-team-brings-hope-and-dedication-to-colorectal-cancer-study/

CHAPTER SUMMARY

>> Key insights

Engagement is crucial. Regardless of their scale, initiatives thrive when they have full engagement from various stakeholders, including internal teams, external collaborators, partners, investors, and customers. When we're working to tackle large-scale challenges like circularity, a shift from hospital-based to home-based healthcare, fintech coordination, or large-scale coordination of advanced manufacturing standards, we need to take engagement to a whole new level and create purpose-driven ecosystems.

>> Key Stuck Points

STUCK POINTS: FRICTION, RESISTANCE, OBSTACLES, CHALLENGES	TOOL TO USE	HOW IT WORKS
We've been taught to create elevator pitches to convince other people to support a new initiative. That's a path to get caught up in our worldviews.	Commitment Narratives	It is grounded in the principle that everyone needs to be a hero in their own story. The Commitment Narrative starts with listening to the person whose support, resources, or participation matters. Then, instead of pitching them, we find common ground between what matters to them and the project we're driving that needs support.
Our projects run risk if they're built for incremental impact. They'll hit a natural plateau once the low-hanging fruit is picked.	Impact Multiplier	Stage a challenge summit focused on multiplying the impact. How might we go global? How might we set a new standard? How might we solve a wicked problem?
When it seems overwhelming to tackle a big challenge, we need to enlist the participation of other companies, partners, collaborators, and co-creators.	Ecosystem Mapper	Map the networks that can be brought to bear to support the initiative. Expand your thinking to include platforms that facilitate the contribution of multiple parties. In cases where something is in the works—like an industry-wide shift from hospitals to home healthcare—bring together several parties and collectively map an ecosystem of purpose.
The most common Stuck Points are the hurdles between incremental growth ambitions and truly transformative innovation.	Transformative Leadership	Your company has no right and wrong; it's up to you to decide where you want to play on the incremental versus transformational spectrum. The Transformative Leadership tool helps you determine if you're settling for a direction that's not ambitious enough. Gather your team to stretch ambitions from incrementalism toward bolder impact. Make sure everyone's on the same page.

>> Key actions

Understand the unique motivations of different stakeholders and create narratives that resonate with each one. Explore ways to tap into opportunities for ecosystem growth and expansion. Map the interconnected parts and players' community to identify opportunities for collaboration and scale. Elevate your level of ambition and brainstorm ideas for bolder, more impactful initiatives.

>> Key questions

The key questions to address in this chapter are:

"What motivates different stakeholders to support our initiative?"

"How can we tap into ecosystem opportunities for growth and impact?"

"Who are the key players in our ecosystem, and how can we engage them effectively?"

>> Commitment

Commit to understanding and addressing the unique motivations of stakeholders, exploring ecosystem growth opportunities, and mapping and collaborating within your ecosystem. Commit to elevating your ambitions and seeking bolder solutions for greater impact.

We need to lead
Ecosystems of Purpose
to tackle big ideas
like home healthcare,
advanced manufac-
turing standards,
fintech cooperation,
and circularity.

STEP 5

ACTIVATE

CREATE A GROWTH FLYWHEEL

GOAL: Enlist commitment, operationalize the initiative, and create an evergreen system to thrive

WHERE MIGHT YOU BE STUCK?

In this chapter, we'll address some of the following Stuck Points—friction, resistance, obstacles, and challenges—that might sound like this:

- "Our project has become an orphan. No one is championing it where it really counts."

- "We're languishing in the execution stage."

- "We've won prizes and accolades, but we're not seeing action."

- "We can't integrate our new project into the top priority corporate strategy."

Unsure where your situation fits in?

Visit www.andreakates.com/diagnostic and take the *From Stuck to Scale* Diagnostic to take stock.

We must eliminate
orphaned projects.

YOU'D THINK THAT with all the elements lined up so well, Intergráficas would be on a sure path toward scale.

They began in a very stuck state as producers of music CDs in a market that was disappearing by the day. But in the Envision stage, they came up with creative ideas for a turnaround. In the Expand phase, the team explored alternative technologies, business models, products, and customer segments outside the music industry. In the Build stage, they built and tested rough versions of products ranging from 3D printing in healthcare to food packaging. Then, in the Engage stage, they forged relationships with suppliers and customers, and won over customers to participate in pilots.

You'd think that their struggles would be over.

Remember when I described the moment when teams give birth to orphans? That's the risk that Intergráficas faced at the end of the Engage stage. Months of hard work were at risk unless they applied the final set of tools focused on Activation to make certain that the early successes led to a sustainable and growing line of business.

We can't take for granted that strong solutions will reach their full potential without attention to four critical questions that Nicolas Cortázar tackled as they embarked on Activate:

- Do we have the people on board to drive this innovation forward with passion, and will they focus relentlessly on going big and bold?

- Are all our bases covered to ensure we execute exceedingly well and remain relevant to our customers over the long run?

- Do we have formal checks to stay ahead of adversity and keep current with our technologies?

- Is our culture built to fuel growth for the new initiative?

Early signs were good that Intergráficas had a winning formula. They had uncovered a match between a superpower they'd almost taken for granted—a six sigma-certified manufacturing process—and a need in a growth industry: food packaging.

Then the pandemic brought drama. First, the restaurants shut down. Bad news.

Next came optimism when the government declared food an essential industry. Good news.

Nicolas weathered the ups and downs of the adjustment to new customers, products, and technical requirements (like temperature control and leakage) that they hadn't needed to worry about when cutting music CDs. But he had a nagging sense that he was missing an element that might doom their growth in the food packaging industry.

He was missing a person. Someone with a relentless focus on going big and bold. A champion whose passion lived in all things concerning packaging possibilities. A leader who would tackle imperatives with gusto.

Enter Gabriel, an experienced operator who loved the company, had a track record for business development, and believed 100 percent in the mission.

It's not necessary to bring in leadership every time there's a shift in corporate direction. But in this case, Gabriel's talents infused the team with vitality and pushed the limits on bold impact.

Nicolas and Gabriel instituted a rigorous and ambitious expansion plan and ignited excitement within the team. They brought customers into the production plant to co-create. They met with future-minded innovators to rethink the fundamentals of sustainable packaging, food delivery, and a customer experience that made Intergráficas' chain-restaurant customers and local food purveyors the favorites of families in the Bogotá area.

But the key to scaling the business was none of those exciting things. Nicolas and Gabriel secured a supply of paper, and when the pandemic hit and it was nearly impossible to secure paper, Intergráficas was all set.

They had smart thinking and good fortune.

The combination of vision, customer traction, logistics, and technology set the path. The addition of a culture of relentless dedication tipped the scales toward growth. The company grew to achieve 6X EBITDA in the couple of years that followed. They overcame chapter after chapter of being stuck and successfully saved jobs, rolled out uncommonly cool food containers, and succeeded in building a flywheel for continued growth.

Intergráficas EBITDA

EBITDA values between 2017 and 2022 (per $1m USD)

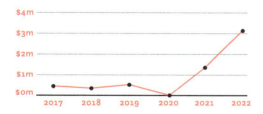

Source: Intergráficas

HOW DO you move the right innovation across the finish line, at scale? None of the tools, techniques, strategies, incubation, and acceleration environments will lead to success if we can't address the underlying challenge: What does it take to move from intention to activation?

Unless we activate our new initiatives, transformation and innovation initiatives become science fair projects: interesting experiments, but lacking real-world relevance.

The ideal way to work with the Activate tools is through a combination of individual work and team discussion. You'll progress your initial ideas from early-stage descriptions to a clearer view of where you believe your organization could increase your impact.

To truly move *From Stuck to Scale*, we need to activate in a new way that moves initiatives onto the front burner. The secret is to integrate the "why" and the "how" into a state of importance for our organizations and ecosystems.

In any application of the Activate stage, moving initiatives across the finish line, at scale, begins here.

Your practical toolkit

The final stage, Activate, teaches you to enlist commitment and operationalize your initiative to ensure it thrives. In this chapter, we have four canvases and a bonus tool for innovation and strategy alignment.

The 4-Beat Activation Story

Takes the initial narrative one step beyond the initial vision. This tool targets one stakeholder and creates a custom version of the initiative that focuses on getting them to move beyond general support toward specific action.

The 4-Quadrant Activation Plan

The four quadrants we used at the beginning of the process also apply in this final stage. We need people to take action to engage others, continue to stretch our vision, tackle logistical and operational issues, and make sure our technology and research are applied at a high standard.

Activation Imperatives

Provides a checkpoint to gauge Headwinds of resistance or challenge, Tailwinds that could accelerate progress, Implications to tackle to get unstuck, and Imperatives—what needs to happen now to move progress forward?

Culture of Activation

Uncovers underlying Beliefs, Actions, Structures, Learning (and unlearning), and Reinforcement that provide a culture to support transformation. A new initiative might be dead in the water if leaders don't know how to manage the organization's culture.

It's time to go back to our 4-Beat Story so we can take our action plan and truly activate it.

BONUS: Strategic Option Evaluation

We have also included a bonus sheet to help align your innovation with your strategy

TOOL: 4-BEAT ACTIVATION STORY

 Purpose

The *From Stuck to Scale* process reinforces the fact that there is no one-size-fits-all elevator pitch that will work for every stakeholder. To enlist support and inspire action, it's critically important to understand what it takes for a specific person, team, or organization to feel committed and to make your initiative a priority. This tool is designed to frame the aspects of your initiative, new line of business, project, or product in terms that inspire others to help drive it forward.

 How to use it + example

The best way to frame a 4-Beat Activation Story is to review your ecosystem map and target decision makers, influencers, and other stakeholders and leaders who are key to your success. Interview them to learn more about their priorities, existing projects, areas where they feel a sense of urgency, and metrics that matter to them in general. Then, match your telling of your project's narrative based on their value, where your initiative could align with their priorities, and how the results could serve their objectives.

Too often, our efforts to activate an initiative fail because we neglect to match stakeholder motivation with how we enlist them. The distinctive value of this tool is that it forces us to articulate the narrative from the stakeholder's perspective.

Most valuable
players to enlist

ACTIVATE | TOOL
4-BEAT ACTIVATION STORY

WHO DO YOU NEED TO ACTIVATE?

Major Food Chain with multiple locations

How to state
the initiative
in the
stakeholder's
terms

BEAT 1: EXPLORATION CHALLENGE STATEMENT

Intergráficas wants to partner with you to create state-of-the-art
packaging that will move from carryout to home delivery

BEAT 2: TRANSFORMATION INITIATIVE

We will set up a series of co-creation sessions in a jointly led innovation
initiative that includes food packaging innovators, food safety experts,
and customers

BEAT 3: IMPACT

Your team will have a forum for brainstorming and building
next-level solutions

BEAT 4: SUCCESS METRICS

· Major Food Chain will have packaging that addresses their own needs:
  carryout, delivery, and potentially other form factors (retail)
· Major Food Chain will have a partner to co-create next-level innovation

What you're
asking the
stakeholder to do

Milestones that
matter to the
stakeholder

Net outcome,
described in
terms that
matter to the
stakeholder

Fill in the sections on the opposite page as follows:

- **WHO DO YOU NEED TO ACTIVATE?** Name a person or a group whose support matters.

- **BEAT 1: EXPLORATION CHALLENGE STATEMENT.** Describe the challenge you'll tackle in terms that they care about.

- **BEAT 2: TRANSFORMATION INITIATIVE.** Outline what you'll do.

- **BEAT 3: IMPACT.** Articulate the short-term and long-term impact.

- **BEAT 4: SUCCESS METRICS.** List specific milestones and metrics that align with the listener's priorities.

ACTIVATE | TOOL
4-BEAT ACTIVATION STORY

WHO DO YOU NEED TO ACTIVATE?

-
-

≫

BEAT 1: EXPLORATION CHALLENGE STATEMENT

-
-

≫

BEAT 2: TRANSFORMATION INITIATIVE

-
-

≫

BEAT 3: IMPACT

-
-

≫

BEAT 4: SUCCESS METRICS

-
-

NOTES

Key takeaway

This process crystallizes the framing of the "ask" into language that speaks directly to the priorities of the person you're trying to enlist. It is focused, personalized, and based on what matters to them.

What to do next

Synthesize all the actions you'll need to do yourself, organize for your team, and orchestrate on behalf of key stakeholders into a 4-Quadrant Activation Plan.

TOOL: 4-QUADRANT ACTIVATION PLAN

 ### Purpose

This canvas synthesizes the top actions required to move an initiative from the initial pilot that you established in the Build stage and then refined in the Engage stage. It is designed as a guide for your team to create timelines, engage more people to support critical components of the activation plan, and bring to life four dimensions of activation that bring an initiative successfully across the finish line.

Activation requires action, commitment, a sense of clarity, and focus. The canvas forces you to frame everything in terms of *doing* rather than *planning*.

 ### How to use it + example

Extract the components of all the 4-Beat Stories you've used to activate the participation of key people.

In considering the Engage quadrant, focus on communication and on enlisting leaders, teams, communities, associations, collaborators, and existing ecosystems.

For the Big Picture quadrant, concentrate on active contributions from leaders from other industries, people involved in policy and governance, and companies who shape big ideas in your field.

In the Logistics quadrant, activate people who drive operations.

Finally, in the Data, Tech, Analysis quadrant, plan your activation of people who manage platforms and experts in advanced technologies, as well as data analysts.

4-QUADRANT ACTIVATION PLAN

ENGAGE

- Create relationships between sales team and restaurant industry teams
- Convene industry innovation design-a-thons that bring together experts in food safety, customer priorities, operations, packaging

BIG PICTURE

- Establish reputation as industry leader in all aspects of food-related packaging
- Catalyze an ecosystem with talent in every aspect of food packaging
- Aspire to lead the industry in sustainable and food-safe materials

LOGISTICS

- Establish briefing sessions to focus on emerging trends in logistics. Include supply chain vendors' paper, materials
- Set up co-creation sessions to advance capabilities in manufacturing and optimizing operations

DATA, TECH, ANALYSIS

- Collaborate with regional universities and trade associations to develop top training in new technologies for current team (AI, robotics, advanced manufacturing)

Step-by-step path to connect with key stakeholders

Core internal steps to achieve goal

Opportunties to harness technology to maximize product potential

Broad statement of change initiative

Your turn: Instructions

Fill in the sections on the opposite page
as follows:

- **ENGAGE.** Include people who are critical
  for buy-in, support, and participation.

- **BIG PICTURE.** Describe the broader vision
  and potential.

- **LOGISTICS.** List the systems and processes
  that must be in place to succeed.

- **DATA, TECH, ANALYSIS.** Include critical
  technologies and analytics.

4-QUADRANT ACTIVATION PLAN

ENGAGE

-
-
-

BIG PICTURE

-
-
-

LOGISTICS

-
-
-

DATA, TECH, ANALYSIS

-
-
-

NOTES

Key takeaway

The focus on action that addresses four distinct components of a plan reinforces the importance of communication, bold vision, operations, and technology. The process of developing the plan as a team forces conversations about what will drive results most effectively and with the greatest impact.

What to do next

Crystallize your activation plan into Activation Imperatives, a quick reminder of where you'll build traction, where you'll face friction, what the implications are, and what you must do next.

TOOL: ACTIVATION IMPERATIVES

 ## Purpose

Create an at-a-glance reference that summarizes critical steps toward progress. It's important to focus on what we can do today to clear obstacles or make bold moves. This canvas optimizes for activation.

 ## How to use it + example

Work with your team to define potential accelerants, obstacles, insights, and must-dos. Use this worksheet to generate a list of possibilities in each category: Headwinds, Tailwinds, Implications, and Imperatives. Then, list the top-priority items in each box.

Potential
issues faced
when
developing
product

Trends or
advantages in
production and
development

ACTIVATE | TOOL
ACTIVATION IMPERATIVES

HEADWINDS

- Hard to shift perception from one industry to another
- Food can be a low-margin business
- Industry culture is not as sexy as music

TAILWINDS

- Expertise in Six Sigma manufacturing
- High-performing teams in sales and design
- Investors can open doors

IMPLICATIONS

- Requires committed and excited leadership team
- Can't be viewed as failing; the market has shifted
- Must pay attention to the culture

IMPERATIVES

- Focus on making new friends and building solid relationships with a new ecosystem
- Double down on the company's DNA as innovators to bring excitement to food packaging

Requirements
to get through
tailwinds and
headwinds

Necessary aspects to
survive/maximize
opportunities

Your turn: Instructions

Fill in the sections on the opposite page as follows:

- **HEADWINDS.** What obstacles, bottlenecks, and resistance do you face?

- **TAILWINDS.** How might you gain traction by tapping into support or resources?

- **IMPLICATIONS.** What snags might come up? Where might you engineer good luck into the process?

- **IMPERATIVES.** What must you do next?

ACTIVATE | TOOL
ACTIVATION IMPERATIVES

HEADWINDS

-
-

∨∨

TAILWINDS

-
-

∨∨

IMPLICATIONS

-
-

∨∨

IMPERATIVES

-
-

NOTES

Key takeaway

Revisit this canvas in weekly sprints with a "tackle and move on" mindset. Activation requires weekly progress and attention to move items forward consistently.

What to do next

To make an initiative stick over the medium and long term, it's important to create habits and practices that reinforce its importance. The Culture of Activation tool looks at specific reinforcements you can make to embed the new project into the processes of the organization.

TOOL: CULTURE OF ACTIVATION

 ## Purpose

Uncover core beliefs that prevent full support of new initiatives. Eliminate orphan projects. Engineer a discipline to instill learning into the organization. Build reinforcement of new habits into the actions and structures of the organization.

 ## How to use it + example

Work as a team (and ideally also with a facilitator) to get to the heart of obstacles and brainstorm ways to reinforce support for a new initiative.

It can be difficult to uncover the underlying belief that drives resistance. Start with what you observe. Next, ask "Why?" multiple times until you dig deeper into motivations and root causes. Then, probe what might be missing or where there might be blind spots.

Example: *You observe a meeting where only one type of person is given the floor to speak.*

Why? *Because they are more experienced. It will save time to start with a past perspective.*

There is a blind spot toward newer employees (perhaps hired from other companies) who could bring novel solutions (for example, machine learning expertise to a manufacturing issue). This blind spot is perpetuated by the belief that only senior engineers can solve problems, thereby excluding the potential for new technology solutions.

Deeper reasons
preventing
progress

Tasks to
reinforce new
priorities

ACTIVATE | TOOL
CULTURE OF ACTIVATION

BELIEFS

· Our heart and soul is music. That's the only way to feel like we have a
dynamic brand

ACTIONS

· Insert innovation into other parts of the company; e.g., contests for
package design

STRUCTURES

· Monthly sizzle metric on excitement generated

LEARNING

· All-star forums, chefs/food, customer-centric packaging innovation

REINFORCEMENT

· Include customer outreach sessions on calendar every month to
consistently gauge their level of engagement with Intergráficas

Workflows and
measurements

Habits built
into team
rewards

Experiences
to stretch
employees'
mindsets

Your turn: Instructions

Fill in the sections on the opposite page as follows:

- **BELIEFS.** Dig into underlying beliefs that might be barriers to the success of the new initiative. You might have to ask "why" a few times to get to the heart of the barriers.

- **ACTIONS.** Work with teams to devise specific actions that will implant the new initiative into people's work plans.

- **STRUCTURES.** To avoid the orphan syndrome, list very specific processes, systems, and metrics that put the new initiative into the KPIs and priorities of the organization.

- **LEARNING.** Experiment with creative ways to reinforce adoption through learning.

- **REINFORCEMENT.** To instill new thinking at the organizational level, be explicit in what teams will do differently to reinforce the growth flywheel.

ACTIVATE I TOOL
CULTURE OF ACTIVATION

BELIEFS

-
-

ACTIONS

-
-

STRUCTURES

-
-

LEARNING

-
-

REINFORCEMENT

-
-

NOTES

Key takeaway

The most important aspect of Activation is making it an organizational habit—instituting specific actions and structures that support new initiatives and keep them from becoming orphans. In the long term, it's critical to engineer learning into the corporate culture: an awareness that mastery of new skills is critical to organizational relevance.

What to do next

This is the last step in the *From Stuck to Scale* process. Debrief with your team using the Strategic Option Evaluation form to assess where you might need to invest extra effort to succeed. To make sure you keep the initiative moving forward with full support of the organization, your team needs to integrate the project's objectives into the company's KPIS or OKRS.

SPOTLIGHT STORY:
ARTHRITIS SOCIETY CANADA
Leading an Ecosystem

When it takes a one-million-person co-creation initiative to drive breakthroughs

Those Zoom calls were numbing. It's hard to remember the months I spent trying to build interpersonal relationships with people during the pandemic using only video calls. Day after day, webinar after webinar, all I could think was, "Does anyone honestly believe we'll build bonds this way?"

One day, I felt the answer to that question was a surprising "yes." I'd been invited to a virtual design thinking workshop to explore future strategies for arthritis. Introducing the video call that day was Trish Barbato, President and CEO of Arthritis Society Canada. Right from the start, I could feel Trish's rapt attention on the community conversation. As the group shared their experiences as arthritis patients, caregivers, medical professionals, members of the public, non-profit staff, and corporate leaders, I could almost see lightbulbs turning on over Trish's head. She was connecting dots in new ways, piecing together the big picture.

After that session, Trish had meetings and conversations just like that with hundreds of people in the arthritis community. She found a provocative and consistent theme emerging: after years of efforts, breakthroughs, and even alliance initiatives focused on arthritis, the level of funding remained unacceptably low relative to the prevalence and economic impact of arthritis. A nationwide Canadian report card confirmed huge gaps in access to care. With six million people directly affected by arthritis just within Canada, the level of government support fell behind support for other diseases. It was also clear that there was a need to engage and empower Indigenous populations.

For Trish, arthritis had reached a tipping point: incremental, siloed efforts would not be sufficient.

One of the people I spoke with put forward a question that haunted me. They asked, "A year from now, will we be having the same conversations, only different versions? What will really have changed?" I realized they were right: this was a problem that called for audacity and boldness.

A few months later, I spoke with Trish about what she learned, and was so captivated by her bold and audacious vision that I began to work with her on an ambitious project: a nationwide Canadian arthritis action plan, co-created with one million people. The goal was to bring together innovation, research, clinical perspectives, awareness, advocacy, and empowerment to provide equitable access to care and forge paths to cures.

Throughout my career, I've been fortunate to be involved in several movements and large-scale initiatives: business transformation, open innovation challenges, product rollouts, and ecosystem projects. However, the ambition of co-creating a plan with such a large group of people brought the notion of scale to a new level.

How might we engage and activate such a large and diverse group to contribute to the creation of the plan? What would be the right set of ingredients to keep people involved once the plan was in place? How might we define metrics along the way, especially as things started to get complicated? Activation doesn't happen with models or pitches: it takes hold when people start to care for their own reasons.

To tackle this huge initiative, we began with the steps I've outlined in this book. We envisioned how the future might look and expanded our perspectives by interviewing people: Gary Bolles shared his experiences building community operating systems; Kelly Stoetzel described the models for the TEDX Clubhouse community; Daniel Kraft from NextMed Health offered insights from XPRIZE challenges; Dr. Eduardo Franco outlined the HPV vaccination initiative that had been so successful in Canada, and so on. Dozens of interviews later, Trish was ready to start building the plan and engage the community in group discussions to inform its foundation.

All of these steps established the groundwork for how Arthritis Society Canada might serve as the backbone organization to establish, nurture, and truly activate the plan. Reflecting on the stories I've shared so far in this book, I recognized a familiar thread to frame our approach to activation. I realized that every example of successful activation underscored the importance of knowing what it will take to get people on board and of figuring out how to motivate everyone in their own way to contribute, provide resources, and help an initiative or a new product or scaleup to grow.

What does it look like to stage an activation session?

For months, Arthritis Society Canada had been convening an integrated scientific and medical advisory group (isMAC) to synthesize insights from multiple technical and healthcare perspectives. Arthritis Society Canada had also formed a community of "champions" that represented national perspectives on patient experience and government advocacy, as well as business, community, and family issues. In Winnipeg, Canada, on a day that turned out to be negative twenty-five degrees Celsius, it was time to bring together isMAC and some of the champions to light the spark of activation.

Trish knew we had to hit all the marks to raise the stakes for everyone in the room, so that everyone would be hooked.

On that cold Tuesday, after the initial welcome, everyone in the room was handed an envelope. Inside was a personal letter from an actual person with arthritis—written just for the recipient.

The letters were heartfelt and had messages like this one (this is a composite of actual patient letters that they received):

Dear Friend,

It's hard to believe that this September, it will be seven years since I have been (knowingly) living with rheumatoid arthritis. It's not an ideal birthday gift to receive at thirty years old, but it's a great reminder each year to be thankful for another spin around the sun.

It feels strange to think back to that thirty-year-old woman who woke up one morning and could not open her hands. I felt alone, overwhelmed, and scared. My family was not familiar with my symptoms (visible and otherwise), and I was not familiar with describing pain and the horrible sensations I was feeling all over my body. Living in a rural community, I found it hard to access healthcare, rheumatologists, and even specialists. I spent hours scouring the internet for information and to access resources. What was wrong with me? Where had it come from? How would I get a diagnosis? One night, I dove deep into the Arthritis Society of Canada website and came across the pages about self-advocacy.

Finally armed with knowledge, I was able to call my doctor and request referrals to people I'd researched, ask about possible medications to try and conditions to be tested for. Arthritis Society of Canada gave me the confidence to take control of my healthcare.

I spent 2020 and the beginning of 2021 doing virtual schooling and working on my health. I found a passion for fitness and a job in public health that I adore. I am proud to be down to a biologic and minimal pain with my disease! Fitness, nutrition, mental wellness, and my biologic are my secret weapons to quality of life.

I want to thank you for your support. Reflecting on my past makes me so optimistic about my future and reminds me how far I've come. I consider myself a success story,

but I know others are not on the same path and they need support now more than ever. We need an action plan to extinguish the fire of arthritis, and I know we'll do it. I am thankful to have a spouse who loves me and fights with me, and I hope my great health continues as we plan to have a family—something I didn't think was possible upon my diagnosis, but that seems more attainable than ever with all I have learned.

As you spend time with other researchers, clinicians, and health professionals this week, I hope my personal story will inspire you to keep working toward a cure for arthritis. I am deeply appreciative of your commitment.

Stay well and stay safe,

MICHELE MCWALTERS,
Port Hope, Ontario, Canada
(reprinted with permission)

After everyone read the letters, the mood was definitely not business as usual. People were touched. It was clear that the work ahead would improve the lives of many people, and everyone in the room had a context for the objectives for the day that didn't require words to describe. They had bought in.

Activation comes when the person in the room feels deeply motivated to take action.

Insights from the Nationwide Arthritis Action Plan as a work in progress

There's a significant road ahead to co-create the plan, gain widespread support, and establish a fully activated ecosystem to change the future course of arthritis and improve the lives of people who are affected by it. What we've learned so far is this: people will be part of the effort for their own reasons, will contribute pieces of a whole, will experience the value and benefit in their own ways. Some people will be interested in public events, others in raising funds or applying AI to a large research database or piecing together a broadly accessible model for care.

The backbone organization will certainly evolve, with Trish shifting roles over the coming months. What's clear is this—successful activation will rely on a combination of concurrent initiatives: challenges orchestrated to solve scientific challenges together, programs designed to touch communities in new ways, campaigns that expand the network of people who care, and technological innovation focused on faster results and more significant impact. Ultimately, those ingredients will add up to improved quality of life and paths to a cure for arthritis.

AT A GLANCE:
ARTHRITIS SOCIETY CANADA

SITUATION	Arthritis Society Canada takes on the task: Co-create a nationwide Arthritis Action Plan with one million people.
FROM STUCK TO SCALE STEP	Activate
WHERE PEOPLE GOT STUCK	Shifting from siloed initiatives toward a collective movement.
HOW THE FROM STUCK TO SCALE APPROACH WORKS BETTER THAN TRADITIONAL STRATEGY	Traditional strategy would create a plan and try to get people to support it. From Stuck to Scale supports activation through a coordinated ecosystem.
BREAKTHROUGH MOMENT	Arthritis Society Canada heard a clear message that the best paths to treatment and paths to a cure for arthritis required collaboration and co-creation.
IMPACT	Early-stage infrastructure toward engaging one million people: core champions group representing major arthritis related organizations. Discussion groups representing national leadership organizations: Indigenous populations, business leaders, government, healthcare professionals, families.
KEY INSIGHT	It's critical to have the backbone organization defined correctly to strike the right balance between central control versus uncoordinated activation efforts.
HOW YOU CAN APPLY THIS	Focus on the 4-Beat Activation Story for each group. What will it take for them to do something, contribute, bring resources to the table?
FINAL TIP	Don't be afraid to let flywheels thrive on their own.

BONUS TOOL: STRATEGIC OPTION EVALUATION

It's valuable to do periodic checks throughout the *From Stuck to Scale* process and the end of an innovation cycle. The Strategic Option Evaluation form is a bonus tool designed to spark conversation during periodic pulse checks.

 Purpose

Align your new initiative with the company's existing strategy.

 How to use it

Take a quick pulse—at a team meeting, strategy retreat, one-on-one—to gauge where people might believe the initiative might be stuck.

Instructions

Fill in the sections on the opposite page as follows:

- **INNOVATION OPTION.** For context, provide a short description of your initiative.

- **STRATEGIC IMPACT.** Quick assessment of whether the initiative is aligned with company priorities.

- **SCALING STAGES.** Ask for a quick pulse check on how each person perceives progress in the five stages of scaling an initiative, divided into two broad categories. The first category looks at whether the initiative is clear on "what to do" and includes Envision, Expand, and Build. The second category looks at whether the initiative is clear on "getting others on board for scale" and includes Engage and Activate.

- **EXECUTION READINESS.** Finally, reflect on the practical considerations required to move the initiative forward. Consider: Is the timing right? Has the Market changed? Do you have the resources lined up? Do you have the talent in place to get the job done?

- **OTHER FACTORS.** Consider other factors that could make a difference in how you move forward. List them and rate them.

STRATEGIC OPTION EVALUATION

INNOVATION OPTION:

	NO	NOT REALLY	WE MIGHT	YES
STRATEGIC IMPACT Is this initiative still well aligned with the company's priorities?				
SCALING STAGES: PART 1 *Envision, Expand, Build* Have we achieved our milestones in "what to do?"				
SCALING STAGES: PART 2 *Engage, Activate* Have we achieved our milestones in "getting others on board for scale?"				
EXECUTION READINESS Is the timing/market right? Are resources lined up? Is the talent in place to get the job done?				
OTHER FACTORS What other factor might matter? _____				
OTHER FACTORS What other factor might matter? _____				

NOTES

Key takeaway

Invite everyone on the leadership team, everyone on the working team, and other stakeholders to provide a quick pulse check. It's a great way to kick off a discussion and pinpoint how to get past places where the initiative might be stuck.

What to do next

Repeat this pulse check throughout the process.

Activation has less to do with writing a perfect plan or getting a whiteboard model right, and more to do with the human element. Simply put, the secret to activation is to set people up to do things that matter to them that also significantly contribute to your project, product, platform, or purpose.

SPOTLIGHT STORY: COPENHAGEN FINTECH
Global Catalyst for Growth

Secrets to a flywheel for collective growth

My mobile rarely rings, but luckily when it happened to ring one summer day, I picked it up. Some colleagues in Denmark had recommended me as a person to help a new ecosystem expand its impact, and here was Thomas Krogh Jensen on the phone, reaching out to share the vision for Copenhagen Fintech, a nascent organization with a remarkable game plan for scaling. They wanted to fuel a thriving global community of banks, innovative scaleups, technology startups, and government leaders and regulators, all based in Denmark.

"Why fintech?" I asked Thomas.

"It started with a viability study on how to build regional economic capacity in Copenhagen. In that report, fintech bubbled to the top. Then, we worked with Startup Genome, a specialty research group, to understand what it would take to create a thriving fintech ecosystem," Thomas explained.

"What do you think it will take?"

"We have to lead with what the Nordics are best at and make sure everyone thrives all along the journey," he answered.

"How do you plan to get people involved?"

"I do my homework to target people I really want, and then I call them on the phone."

He had me.

A couple of months after that initial call with Thomas, I flew to Copenhagen for an advisory board meeting and the Copenhagen Fintech conference. In the years since that visit, I have watched that nascent organization progress from its early ambitions to what it is today: a highly activated global hub that supports innovation within large banks, a catalyst for growth for companies like Chainalysis and Pleo, and a connector for organizations like Danish-based Saxo Bank, global brands like Mastercard, and other regional hubs in Asia and Europe.

Here's the story of what I learned from Thomas about activating a community and keeping it flourishing over time.

The beginnings of Copenhagen Fintech

In 2015, representatives from the Danish government, associations, and corporate leaders commissioned a study to address a burning question: Might Copenhagen be a viable location to build a cluster of economic opportunities related to fintech?

The research pointed to a "yes, but." Copenhagen had several elements that might support a fintech cluster: a strong digital infrastructure, a good quality of life for young talent, and political and regulatory support. However, the headwinds were also strong: a lack of track record in nurturing scaleups, gaps in entrepreneurial experience, unproven history in accessing investment capital, and competition from other geographies that had already established fintech clusters.

Well aware of the challenges, Copenhagen Fintech was founded in 2016 with Thomas at the helm. Right from the start, the organization reflected the intersection of interests represented in their founding participants, including government, associations, corporations, public sector groups and, eventually, a new sector that they would establish as the vehicle to bring innovation to market: a community of startups.

They established guiding principles, KPIs, and an ethos favoring swift action over exhaustive planning. However, the most compelling priorities for thriving focused on global connectedness and ensuring that people in the Copenhagen Fintech ecosystem constantly served others with substantive contributions.

The nine guiding principles at play, by Thomas Krogh Jensen

1. **Create a magnetic vision:** Finding a purpose to unite behind.

2. **Define what makes a success:** Setting goals and taking action.

3. **Become the natural epicenter:** Supplying what the ecosystem demands.

4. **Get commitment through funding:** Co-financing to create engagement.

5. **Become a mediator and broker:** Understanding needs to make matches.

6. **Build your community and followership:** Managing relationships with intimacy.

7. **Build a versatile and small team:** Leveraging the team and community.

8. **Make communication a strategic priority:** Becoming the authority.

9. **Think and go global from the start:** Becoming the Nordic portal to the world.

"It's not enough to write a check or attend a conference. From the start, Copenhagen Fintech knew we needed to get everyone to do more, take more dramatic action, proactively bring the rest of the community to new levels, and make sure that everyone felt like they were part of the collective success . . . 100 percent of the time."

THOMAS KROGH JENSEN, CEO Copenhagen Fintech

Two secrets to activation: Renew relationships regularly, and take action on behalf of other people

Early in the relationship with Thomas, he suggested I speak with JF Gauthier, founder of Startup Genome, to understand their secret sauce for sustained growth that Thomas mastered in his early days working to establish Copenhagen Fintech. Startup Genome compared communities that formed and stagnated with communities that continued to thrive. The two factors that turned out to matter most were global connectedness—genuine relationships with peers all over the world—and a willingness to take action: to introduce, get involved, collaborate, fund, and participate.

Copenhagen Fintech has taken Startup Genome's advice to heart. They are constantly moving, renewing global connections in virtually every region. Copenhagen Fintech's network is engineered for action. It's not enough to write a membership check. Thomas favors swift action over exhaustive planning. He favors doing over networking. Based on the nine guiding principles, the advice on global connectedness, and a bias toward proactively helping other companies to succeed, the community has given rise to startups and scaleups covering a broad range of financial services: banking, lending, payments, blockchain, insurance, corporate infrastructure, embedded finance, investments, and analytics.

Copenhagen Fintech has built an extensive community globally from their base in Copenhagen. The Nordic ecosystem has produced global leaders in fintech such as Chainalysis, Pleo, Doconomy, and Klarna, to mention a few. Copenhagen Fintech's investor network includes eighty CVCs and VCs investing from pre-seed to series levels.

Envision: Setting the ambitious North Star

Copenhagen Fintech began with a vision of unity and global connectivity. Recognizing the untapped potential within Denmark's scattered fintech landscape, the board's ambition was to establish Copenhagen as a significant global financial player focused on technology-driven innovation. A study in 2015 highlighted Copenhagen's strengths and the pressing need for action to harness the wave of fintech growth for job creation and economic advancement. This led to the first guiding principle: Create a magnetic vision establishing a unifying purpose to rally stakeholders around a shared goal.

Expand: Creating a global network from a Nordic base

With aspirations to transcend its geographical limitations, Copenhagen Fintech's strategy was to not be the largest, but the most globally connected hub. It leveraged Denmark's strong digital infrastructure and embraced a "New Nordic" approach, blending public support and private entrepreneurship to serve as a magnet for global partnerships. This strategy reflects the second principle by defining what makes a success, setting clear goals, and taking decisive action to become a global fintech nexus.

Build: Leveraging lessons to foster growth

Building on lessons learned, Copenhagen Fintech focused on real-time demands, rapidly implementing programs that directly addressed the needs of startups and established financial entities. They honed a model that balanced public and private funding, ensuring flexibility and independence while driving commitment from its stakeholders. The ecosystem's growth was tracked against robust KPIs, illustrating a clear trajectory of success from inception. Their approach to becoming the natural epicenter and supplying the ecosystem's demands was pivotal.

Engage: Fostering a community-centric ecosystem

At the heart of Copenhagen Fintech's ethos was the concept of "eco" over "ego." They created an inclusive community by focusing on the collective good, fostering a culture of collaboration and open innovation. This approach resonated deeply within the ecosystem, allowing for a blend of corporate know-how with startup agility and creativity, thus establishing a thriving environment for fintech innovation. This mirrors the principle of building your community and followership, and managing relationships with intimacy.

Activate: Embracing action to drive systemic change

Copenhagen Fintech's key to activation lies in *doing* rather than over-planning. This philosophy led to systemic change through strategic initiatives likened to strategically placed acupuncture needles. By relinquishing control, Copenhagen Fintech empowered all participants in the ecosystem to contribute, which was critical in cultivating a dynamic and responsive environment.

AT A GLANCE:
COPENHAGEN FINTECH

SITUATION	Copenhagen Fintech has ambitions to fuel a growing global community based in Denmark.
FROM STUCK TO SCALE STEP	Activate
WHERE PEOPLE GOT STUCK	Keeping the ecosystem engaged and designing mechanisms for ongoing collective action.
HOW THE FROM STUCK TO SCALE APPROACH WORKS BETTER THAN THE TRADITIONAL STRATEGY	Traditional community-building can feel like information broadcasts and conferences. By contrast, true activation comes from designing and deploying a steady stream of collaborative initiatives.
BREAKTHROUGH MOMENT	Copenhagen Fintech realized they needed to be alert to the needs of their member companies and help them overcome obstacles: product creation, customer retention, and market-building. Then, member companies could collaborate with others to amplify everyone's growth opportunities.
IMPACT	The Nordic ecosystem has produced global leaders in fintech such as Chainalysis, Pleo, Doconomy, and Klarna. Copenhagen Fintech's investor network includes eighty cvcs and vcs investing from pre-seed to series levels.
KEY INSIGHT	Interpersonal trust is earned through every interaction.
HOW YOU CAN APPLY THIS	Evaluate the time you invest in nurturing personal relationships, both local and global.
FINAL TIP	As you scale, don't forget to pick up the phone.

CHAPTER SUMMARY

>> Key insights

Moving innovation initiatives from intention to activation is crucial for success. Without activation, these initiatives can become little more than science fair projects.

>> Key Stuck Points

STUCK POINTS: FRICTION, RESISTANCE, OBSTACLES, CHALLENGES	TOOL TO USE	HOW IT WORKS
The worst place to stall is after a successful pilot that got you buy-in. The danger is: there's a big difference between a stakeholder *supporting* your initiative versus making it a priority, rolling up their sleeves, and taking action.	4-Beat Activation Story	Targets one key stakeholder and frames the initiative in terms that matter most to them. Rather than presenting a standard pitch, the bias is toward custom messages and specific action.
Early in our process, we learned that nothing takes flight without four types of effort: 1) keeping people contributing, 2) continuing to stretch the bounds of possibility, 3) solid logistics and operations, and 4) technical chops. If we don't nail activation in all four quadrants, we may hit a doom cycle.	4-Quadrant Activation Plan	No plan works without four categories of action. This tool serves as an implementation check: Are our instructions clear? Are all the execution bases covered? Are we diligently ensuring everyone hits their marks?
Just as we've won prizes and accolades and engaged an extended support network, suddenly we're blindsided by headwinds. New forces arise: a pandemic, a regulatory shift, widespread acceptance of AI. That's a signal to gather supporters and create emergency action agendas.	Activation Imperatives	Every month, the leadership team checks in using this tool. What's changed? Which are the most important actions we must do right now? Where do we need to shift our focus to make sure we maintain momentum?
We talked about the tragedy of orphaned projects: initiatives that enjoy early support but that don't survive the journey back into the mothership (if it's coming from an incubator). That's why it's so important to proactively construct a culture that will make sure your initiative thrives.	Culture of Activation	There are subtle forces that come into play when we ask people to take on something new. Sometimes old habits return, undermining progress. Other times, we have unconscious preferences for the status quo (e.g., preferring music over food packaging). It takes new habits, reinforced by leaders, to guard against backsliding and fan the flames of innovation.

>> Key actions

Craft a narrative that resonates with stakeholders' priorities and motivations. Create a comprehensive plan that outlines actions for different dimensions of activation. Establish habits and practices within the organization to reinforce the importance of the initiative.

>> Key questions

The key questions to address in this chapter are:

"What motivates stakeholders to commit to our initiative, and how can we frame it accordingly?"

"What actions are required to move our initiative forward, and how can we address obstacles and leverage support?"

"How can we create a culture of activation and continuous learning within our organization?"

>> Commitment

Commit to creating a comprehensive activation plan and identifying and prioritizing key actions to overcome challenges. Commit to embedding a culture of activation and learning within the organization to ensure long-term success.

We can't take a back
seat when there's
so much potential to
apply our ingenuity
and humanity to make
our world a much
better place. Together,
we've got this.

CONCLUSION

YOU'LL BE PLEASED to know that Nicolas Cortázar leveraged his strategic experience with Intergráficas to become a strategy leader with ... yes, Warner Music Group, where he's back in the music industry. He's able to apply the tools and track record to have an even bigger impact with a much larger organization, building a high-performing and interconnected ecosystem that brings entertainment to the next level. And Intergráficas continues to thrive with healthy EBITDA and a super-charged culture. The doubting board—including "Dr. No"—have all been converted to raving fans. Customers like KFC have become true collaborators.

Nicolas and I stay in close touch, brainstorming new models and elevating the team's ambitions to keep ahead of change.

For me, the most exciting result I've witnessed is the impact that getting unstuck has had on the people Nicolas has worked with over the years. Once the mindset shifted and people had tools to build true growth flywheels together, they have been able to tackle opportunities as they landed on the doorstep: How might we apply AI to assist our team? How might we go global? How might we take on a new challenge with our partners?

That's the mindset that drives a thriving company. That's the skillset that builds impact at scale.

As you begin your journey *From Stuck to Scale*, look for examples of teams you admire. Send them a note. Schedule a chat. Build your own body of evidence based on how others have done it. Through this connection, we can build thriving networks of collaboration that can change the world.

AT THE beginning of the book, I asked if you'd ever experienced moments of feeling stuck: eager to explore a new direction, but for whatever reason feeling like your tires were spinning in the muck.

Throughout *From Stuck to Scale*, I've outlined specific strategies to jumpstart progress at every stage of stuck. I've introduced you to people who have inspired me and taught me that great leaders today bring forward a combination of ingenuity, creativity, technical chops, and conscience. Through a steady progression of skills and a systematic application of the tools I've created and included in this book, you'll be prepared to bring your important ideas to market, inspire an ecosystem of partners, and make the world a better place.

When we get it right, we can bring ideas that matter to many people.

That's the power of getting unstuck.

Remember the story I shared about the frustrating experience when I was CEO of the SaaS company, watching the accidental creation of orphan projects? You'll recall that we hosted 13,000 teams whose mission was to commercialize innovation, apply new technologies to unmet customer needs, and create new lines of business at scale. I lost a twenty-dollar bet, guessing wrong about what it took to grow thriving innovation initiatives, and inadvertently seeding dozens of projects that would get stuck at various points in their development.

What would I do differently today, using the tools I created and shared in this book?

- I'd focus on the flywheels, not the Petri dishes. It was so tempting to be lured into believing that bright shiny objects would translate to thriving businesses. But the truth is, invention alone isn't sufficient to create a business.

- I'd apply a Where Are You Stuck Diagnostic (www.andreakates.com/diagnostic) frequently. It's critical to have early warning signs of trouble, but traditional tools like IRR and guesstimates like TAM and SAM don't steer us toward the necessary interventions.

- I'd hand every team this book and say, "Try this."

RECENTLY, I was honored to give the keynote address for the MIT Foundry Fellows, a group of global leaders who were about to return to their home countries to carry forth the knowledge they'd received in the program. The Executive Director, Dina Sherif, asked me to include a message that would crystallize the MBA insights and highlight a call to action.

To prepare, I watched dozens of commencement addresses by people like Michelle Obama, Randy Pausch, Bono and Shonda Rimes. I thought about the *From Stuck to Scale* themes I was working on.

I pictured all these inspiring leaders from the MIT graduating class returning to their communities and countries to build infrastructure, establish employment opportunities, and influence governments.

To frame my call to action, I decided that the best message would come from Batman. I resisted the temptation to focus the speech on the individual talents of a superhero, and instead compelled the graduates to consider the combined impact of two characters whose talents were multiplied when they learned to work together toward a greater goal—leaders who could leverage their circle of trust and create what I call a Circle of Must: Batman and Commissioner Gordon.

Batman's motivation is based on fighting evil. Commissioner Gordon's motivation is keeping Gotham City safe. It's only by combining their individual "commitment narratives" that Batman and Commissioner Gordon, together—tapping into their mutual respect, track record and trust—activate a Circle of Must. Flash the Bat-Signal, and Batman will be there in an instant.

At its heart, *From Stuck to Scale* equips all of us to rally exactly that type of call to action.

But thankfully, we don't have to be superheroes to drive transformation. Leaders who build strong ecosystem relationships create that same Circle of Must to bring out the best in everyone, underscore the collective importance of a critical initiative, inspire people to take action, and together make the world a better place.

Together, we've got this.

WHAT NOW?

SHARE THE BOOK with others, hold a summit, workshop with your teams to get unstuck, or reach out if you need a fresh perspective and coaching.

Do it yourself or do it with us. We've got tools to get you started. Check out the Bonus Resources section for how to get involved.

MORE WAYS TO GET UNSTUCK

Scale the message

Need to give inspiration to many? Andrea can tailor content in a speech that will give your audience actionable tools to use immediately.

Custom workshops

Need more personalized attention? Whether in-person or virtual, for a half day or multiple days, get an objective, outside view with a custom-tailored program for your team designed to get you unstuck now.

Individual attention

Need a little one-on-one time to talk through your problem? Book a 45-minute session with Andrea through her website.

Consulting projects

Want Andrea to advise your company or project? Get in touch through the website!

www.andreakates.com

SOME OF MY FAVORITE STORIES

Pay it forward

We're starting a movement of like-minded people to continue to learn together. Build community. Start a movement. Share your experiences, coach your teams, and speak to leaders in your company and your ecosystem.

What's your story?

Let's amplify your stories so you can help our global community. Reach out to me at andrea@andreakates.com or on LinkedIn.

AI adoption

"Andrea's example of how Arthritis Society Canada used AI to tackle a nationwide health-care problem gave me the clarity I needed to embrace AI for our organization."

Attendee at **LG INNOFEST**

Build an ecosystem

"We've been talking about building an eco-system for months but didn't know how to get started. Learning about how Copenhagen Fintech built their community was exactly what I needed to make our first move."

Attendee at **RUFORUM AFRICA**

Lead a movement

"We were inspired to learn how Rappi went from delivering sandwiches on bicycles to becoming the largest omnichannel platform in Latin America. Monday morning, back at the office, we rolled up our sleeves and thought much bigger."

Attendee at **DISRUPTIVE INNOVATION NETWORK UK**

Bring new technology to market

"I'd attended Techstars, won pitch campaigns and done pilots in the past, but Andrea's tools made us realize we needed to stop pitching and start building infrastructure partners to take it to the next level."

MIT FOUNDRY FELLOWS

Intrapreneurs + innovation

"We all got stuck at some point in our inno-vation process but didn't know how to dig out. From *Stuck to Scale* takes over where lean startup, design thinking, and agile software models stop. We now have practical diagnostics to figure out what's wrong and how to fix it."

Client at **FUJITSU**

BONUS RESOURCES

NEED A SHORTCUT TO KNOW WHERE YOU'RE STUCK?

TAKE THE WHERE ARE YOU STUCK DIAGNOSTIC: This three-minute Diagnostic SHOWS where you're stuck and GIVES YOU tools to start making progress immediately.

www.andreakates.com/diagnostic

DOWNLOADS

To help you and your teams apply the principles of this workbook, you can use the code provided below and download all the exercises in a PDF from our website.

https://andreakates.com/buyfsts_worksheets

Code: WORKSHEETS4ME

Want the latest updates on tools and shared stories from our community? Sign up for news and updates at:

www.andreakates.com/connect

Here to help. Get in touch at andrea@andreakates.com

CONNECT WITH ME

LinkedIn/IN/ANDREAKATES

@ANDREA.KATES

ACKNOWLEDGMENTS

WITH APPRECIATION to people who supported the development of this book...

The leaders highlighted in the book: Nicolas Cortázar from Intergráficas and now at Warner Music Group; Mohi Ahmed from Shimizu; Guido Becher from Rappi; Antonia Soler Blasco from Hilti; James Rogers at Mayo Clinic; Trish Barbato from Arthritis Society Canada; Alex Tsado from Ahura.ai, Dina Sherif from MIT Center for Development and Entrepreneurship; Joe Kent, Angela Rosenquist and Dan Peach from InnovAsian; Bunmi Akinyemiju from Greenhouse Capital; Thomas Krogh Jensen from Copenhagen Fintech; from the Edison Awards/Latimer Fellows community, Frank Bonafilia, Florian Schattenmann, and Bob Maughon; from Hilti, Michael Neidow; and from Fieldwire, Yves Frinault and Javed Singha.

John Metselaar for the inspiring foreword and the chance to collaborate and field test material with The Conference Board.

Lauren Nguyen Cohen and Neil Cohen for your vision, brilliance, and 24/7 commitment.

Strategy colleagues: Gary Bolles, Stephen Shapiro, Ennis Olson, Lars Ib, Stuart Crainer/Thinkers50, Jonathan Hoffberg, Jorge Arango, Kathleen Nielsen, Ed Morrison, Jennifer He, Dan Toma, Daniel Kraft/ NextMedHealth, Emily Watkins, Joe Brady, Chrestina Ib, Barbara Annis, Kent Lawson, Ed Hansen, Sharon Richmond, Jay Kothari, Søren Juul Jorgensen, Elise St. John, Chenyang Xu, Scott Kirsner, Diana Joseph, Hans Balmaekers/Innov8rs, Tendayi Viki, Jim Euchner, Christian Crews, Heidi Kleinmaus, Pete Comeau, Mario Hernandez, Michelle DeAngelis, Sheila Thorne, Elizabeth Luff, Becky Turner, Jim Chappell, Ben Wilkinson, Zeev Neuwirth, and Russ Lebovitz.

The people who I worked with to formulate the key concepts in *From Stuck to Scale*—Ford: Jaime Foucher and Michelle Tilley; Fujitsu: Ryoma Ohashi, Dave Marvit, and Barry Katz; Tata: Rajiv Navekar; KK Wind: Rene Balle.

Peer support: The Writers Kollectiv at Shack15; Innovation Research Exchange and fellow members of the Research-Technology Management journal Board of Editors: Tammy McCausland, Yat Ming Ooi; John Monks, Nicole Yershon, Changemakers community, Cindy White, Antonia Nichols, Dorian Webb, Pascal Coppens, David Rasson, Julie Morris, Melissa Cohen and the DIY community, Seth Godin's community, Martin Hopp, Alex Popov, Rebecca Alcon, Alex Pesjak, Cris Beswick, Tim Leberecht, Kelly Stoetzel, Saul Kaplan, Sam McAfee, Valerie Conn, Nelly Colapinto, Nick Lupinetti, Navrina Singh, Andreas Sjostrom, Yumi Prentice, Dave Hersh, Simon Pole, Steve Moskowitz, National Association of Manufacturers, Thomas Poedenphant, and Henry Coutinho-Mason.

Diagnostic, technology platform, and tools: Angel Ramirez/cuemby.com, Matthew Morris, brand management: Natalia Briceño Dreyfus and PR: Julie Brewer.

Visionary publishing house, Grammar Factory Publishing: Scott MacMillan, Olivia Jeorges, Julia Kuris, Setareh Ashrafologhalai, and Ania Ziemirska.

THIS IS MY WHY

When I read a book, I want to know what makes the author tick. For me, work has always been about helping people discover better tools to bring important ideas to market. I started my career working with pioneers in industries like mobility, telecommunications, healthcare, hospitality, manufacturing, technology, and retail. It was an era when revolutions were quietly arriving in waves. E-commerce shook up brick-and-mortar retail. Deregulation hit telecom. Digital tools came on the scene and quickly became pervasive. The buzz was all about business innovation wins.

What stopped me in my tracks, time and time again, was the number of ideas that died on the vine after coming so close to succeeding.

Conventional thinking can't solve unconventional problems

What I realized is that conventional tools didn't prepare people for all of the newness coming at us. It was clear that so many of the frameworks we were used to were a lousy fit for the change around us. For example, Six Sigma helped with efficiency but wasn't a great match for commercializing innovation.

I committed to creating better tools and piecing together elements of open innovation, design thinking, and blue ocean strategy. I wrote a book, *Find Your Next,* that documented the first piece of the puzzle: How do we take advantage of change?

About ten years ago I took on the CEO role for a SaaS software company designed to bring the lean startup principles to scale. I was lucky to work with the National Science Foundation, NIH, DARPA, as well as university researchers and companies like Intel, Nasdaq, and Mayo Clinic. It was exciting to be part of the journey of 13,000 teams that were all dedicated to bringing inventions across the finish line, and frustrating to witness the thousands of important innovations that landed on the cutting room floor.

So, I challenged myself to figure it out and developed original tools, working with clients at Ford, Fujitsu, Intergráficas, KK Wind, Tata, and Unispace as well as universities like Business Institute Denmark and MIT.

Enabling purpose and progress

Today, I'm lucky to travel the world helping people get unstuck so that great ideas can reach the people who need them. I've been fortunate to speak at well-known global events including the TED main stage, the Aspen Ideas Festival, the CXO Forum in Tokyo, Dubai 2020, the Edison Awards for global innovation, Rueda de Innovación (Bogotá) and RUFORUM in Africa.

Lifting people and organizations to fulfill their purpose is what fuels me—this is my "why." I love to collaborate, co-create, bring movements to life, and apply innovation and technology to tackle big challenges, which is why I enjoy my roles as Senior Fellow with The Conference Board and MIT Entrepreneur-in-Residence, Sloan School of Managament, Legatum Center for Entrepreneurship and Development.

Every place I visit, I'm struck by the power of crystallizing business insights from one leader's experience into stories that can help others.

When I'm not on the road, I'm in San Francisco, where I'm continually inspired by the beauty, the openness of the people, and the connections from home to the world.

I hope this toolkit helps you clear the path to the next step or toward your broader vision. I'm here to help, so send me a note to tell me how you're doing, or share your stories with me so that I and others can also learn from your experience.

What's your story?

With gratitude,

ANDREA

SHARE YOUR STORY

TOPIC

FROM STUCK
TO SCALE STEP

HOW YOU
WERE STUCK

HOW THE
FROM STUCK
TO SCALE TOOLS
AND SKILLS
HELPED YOU

BREAKTHROUGH
MOMENT

IMPACT

KEY INSIGHT

NOTES

NOTES

NOTES

NOTES

NOTES

NOTES

NOTES

NOTES

NOTES